JOHN B. KEANE

OWL
SANDWICHES

BRANDON

First published 1985
Brandon Book Publishers Ltd.
Dingle, Co. Kerry, Ireland
and 51 Washington Street,
Dover, New Hampshire 03820, U.S.A.

Acknowledgements are due to the editors of the following publications in which some of the essays in this book first appeared: the *Boston Irish News*, the *Evening Herald*, *The Kingdom* and the *Limerick Leader*.

Design by Brendan Foreman and Steve MacDonogh
Typesetting by Setleaders Limited, Dublin
Printed and bound by Billings Ltd.

To Sally and Oliver

Contents

Those Hairs Thou Hast

Shakespeare, while a man of many words, was a fellow of few hairs. Atop his benign countenance was a cranium as bald and shiny as the proverbial billiard ball. He was adequately compensated, of course, by the most artistically designed of moustaches and by a daintily trimmed, tapering beard but his pate proper played host to not a single, solitary hair. At the rear of his noble napper was a curling yet disciplined mane. You might say his baldness was framed in hair and this was a blessing in many ways for Shakespeare lived at a time when the common or garden flea was yet to be intimidated and annihilated by the scourge of DDT and this was surely a blessing in itself. In those days a head without fleas was like Hamlet without the prince and it is to that same Hamlet we will now look in an endeavour to enlighten the gentle reader.

> Those hairs thou hast and their adoption tried
> Grapple them to thy poll with hoops of steel.

He is a wise man who would ponder well this slight variation of Polonius's advice to his son. For some years now I have been steadily forfeiting hair to the advancing years but not until last week did old Father Time thin my scant thatch to such a degree that unless drastic steps are taken I will have no hair at all at the end of the year.

God be with the days when doting aunts and other female relations would ask me to give them a curl from the dense locks which adorned my youthful head. I thought then that I would never see a poor day with regard to hair. Many a time and oft was the floor of the barber shop strewn black with my gartered fringes and curls. I have lost count of the appreciative gasps tendered by those who awaited their turn on stools at my rear.

"Will I take much off the top?" The question was put to me a thousand times. So burdened was I with tresses at my summit that all I would do was shrug to indicate that it was immaterial to me how much was taken off. Indeed I used often say, "Let the bone be your guide," safe in the certain knowledge that my thatch would be completely restored in a matter of days. Now, alas, this is no longer the case. I need every rib I have and I wince when I hear the preparatory snips of the barber's shears.

It is not that I mourn the loss of all the thousands of ribs down the denuding decades for it is true to say that I have presently little use for them, there now being no need for a preening display. I already have a mate and it gives me all I can do to cope with her. I truly appreciate the hairs that have remained faithful. My regret is that I cannot guarantee a future to these fine old retainers who have served me so well for so long.

There is a female friend of mine who is married to a man who is as bald as an apple. He was bald when she fell in love with him and she assures me that she never once looked at his head while they were courting. She was too engrossed with his beautiful blue eyes.

In my time I have tried everything from medicated shampoos to natural colour restorers. Lately I have taken to applying hair foods but instead of fattening and toning up the hairs they seem to affect them so perversely that they cannot withstand even minor investigation from an ordinary pocket comb. They wilt and die after a few days feeding even when that same feeding is reinforced by hair vitamins.

The odd thing is that I have never had so many hairs in my nostrils and I am tempted to ask if the vitamins and hair foods are being selfishly gobbled up by the hairs of the nose whilst the hairs of the head languish on the outside like the íochtars of the litter. Often when I address young children they turn to their parents and say, "Look he has hair in his nose." I wonder if there is some way that these nose hairs could be transferred to the top of my head. Could they be grafted for instance?

In addition to growing fewer my hairs are also growing greyer with the odd one here and there turning white although it is only fair to recall that my maternal grandmother used always say in this respect that a cabbage was no good till it was white.

Alas sometimes with the whitening of the head comes dotage. Who recalls Lewis Carroll's "Father William"?

"You are old Father William," the young man said
"And your hair has become very white
And yet you incessantly stand on your head
Do you think at your age it is right?"
"In my youth," Father William replied to his son,

"I feared it might injure the brain,
But now that I'm perfectly sure I have none
Why I do it again and again."

I have no objection to grey hairs or indeed to baldness. What I object to is people coming up to me and saying, with surprise, "My God, you're nearly bald," or "I'd hardly know you you're so grey."

They make these incredulous comments as though they expected man to retain both his hair and the colour of his hair from his youth to his old age. It does not matter to them that they themselves are grey or bald. One complementary aspect of baldness is that the person in question will never again be grey or white. Luckiest of all is he who is born bald because what he never had he will never miss.

I would not be making these observations at all but for the present, unprecedented advance of baldness, although I tend maybe to make light of the matter just as the vanishing hairs are making light of my head. Then I console myself with the thought that should all my hair abandon my pate my expenses will be considerably cut down. There will be no need to replace that semi-toothless pocket comb, no need to purchase hair oil or hair cream and no need to visit the barber. Look at the time it would spare. For every form of loss in this world there is some form of compensation and I may console myself with the prospect of no colds in the head since there is no more hair to get wet.

An Invisible Dog

One morning as I was walking along New York's Fifth Avenue I beheld a most unusual sight. The time was mid-September. The temperature, according to the hotel porter, was ninety degrees and there wasn't a puff of wind. No one would deny that it had the makings of a tough day for dogs.

However, I am happy to say that the amazing sight which I beheld had to do with the alleviation of suffering in mutts of all shapes and sizes. There is no doubt but the Americans are a canine-orientated race. They do for their dogs what we would only do for humans. That is why there was a beautifully designed doggy trough outside a major store, dead smack in the middle of Fifth Avenue. There was no such trough for humans. If a human wanted to quench his thirst he had to hand out a dollar to an orange juice vendor. The sidewalks of New York are littered with such vendors. There they stand at every street corner squeezing fresh oranges into jugs. They pour from the jugs into glasses of the six ounce variety which is less than a third of a pint. The orange juice is absolutely pure and you can have it chilled or at prevailing temperatures.

While I stood looking at the doggy trough a tall man wearing a Stetson stopped as well. He surveyed the trough bemusedly.

"They look after their dogs here," I said. Immediately an affrighted look appeared in his eyes and he vamoosed like a scalded cat into the huge throngs which move up and down the vast sidewalks of the most crowded avenue in the whole wide world. I had committed the cardinal sin. I had addressed a stranger out of doors in New York. Most people who walk up and down Fifth Avenue are from out of town. They've been brainwashed about the possibilities of being mugged although statistics show that there is no mugging on Fifth Avenue except on isolated occasions. It is a lot safer than our own O'Connell Street.

Fifth Avenue is where you are pestered by advertising. Handbills are being thrust at people from one end of the day to the other. Out of work actors and models earn from two to five dollars an hour for distributing catalogues and handbills. For this they

10

have to dress up as clowns and paint their faces outrageously white. Some really hassle people into taking their handouts. An actor friend told me he did this kind of work regularly. If you don't perform you're booted out without mercy. In short you earn your oats or get out.

On the morning in question the avenue looked well. Hundreds entered and left Saint Patrick's Cathedral which is the very hub of the avenue. Most of these prayed for long-suffering Cardinal Cooke, since deceased. On my way back to 44th Street after leaving the cathedral I beheld another unusual sight. A young lady was distributing free packs of cigarettes from a large satchel strapped on to her shoulder. On the ground was another satchel filled with packs of this new brand. Free packs were pressed upon everybody and I noticed that several people returned a second time to claim another pack. Most people, however settled for one.

Then along came a young man. He accepted a pack of cigarettes but before moving on he surveyed the full satchel on the ground. Without as much as by your leave he lifted the satchel. He did it unhurriedly, as though the satchel were his. When the girl protested he lifted a clenched fist.

"You want I should smash your face in," he shouted.

"Oh dear, no," she answered with the most disarming of smiles.

The man sauntered off with the satchel and another short paragraph was finished in the annals of Fifth Avenue. Instead, however, of returning to 44th Street I followed him from a safe distance. This was easy with the satchel to identify him. He walked and walked until, eventually, for reasons best known to himself he discarded the satchel, giving it a mighty kick after he had placed it on the ground and filled his pockets with free packs.

When next I looked up at a street sign I saw that I was passing 51st Street. At the corner there was an establishment which was as close to a huckster's shop as anything I had seen since arriving in New York. I daresay my mind was partially on dogs at the time because the one notice that was sticking out a mile on the window had the following, unbelievable announcement: "Invisible Dogs. Two Dollars."

Underneath was a wire lead attached to a plastic collar. This was my sort of scene. Without further ado I entered. Behind the only counter which the shop boasted was an incredibly small man without a rib of hair on his head. A pencil-thin moustache divided his distinctly Jewish nose from his small mouth.

"Yeah?" he asked when I approached the counter.

"What kind of invisible dogs you got?" I asked respectfully.

"I got all kinds," he said and lifted a chain and collar from a nearby peg, "but this one is special and he don't cost nothin' extra. You got kids?

"Sure," I told him, "I got kids."

"He loves kids," the baldheaded man assured me."

"What's his breed?" I asked.

"He ain't got no breed," said the baldheaded man. "He's just special like I told you."

"Is he housebroken?" I asked matter of factly.

"Well I'll tell ya," said the baldheaded man. "He's been here six weeks and he ain't peed yet."

"Some dog," I said. "I'll take him."

Reverently he took the dog in his arms and brought him outside the counter where he placed him on the shop floor. I handed over two dollars.

"You treat him good now, you hear," he cautioned.

"What's his name?" I asked.

"Name is Fred, same as his old man," I was told. I led him out on to the street and I swear I heard a bark but maybe the small, baldheaded man was a ventriloquist.

I looked at my watch. Almost one o'clock. I had an appointment for lunch with a Greek at the New York Athletic Club. I unleashed the dog and gave him his freedom. He went yelping down the street.

The Long Stagger

In the year nineteen twenty-seven William Harrison Dempsey, otherwise known as Jack Dempsey, was floored by Gene Tunney in their rematch for the world heavyweight boxing championship which Dempsey had, the year before, lost to Tunney. So began the saga of the Long Count. Dempsey, in his anxiety to beat the daylights out of Tunney, who was on the canvas in the sixth, failed to return to a neutral corner until several seconds had elapsed thereby giving Tunney the breather he needed to beat the count and hold on to his title.

Of lesser fame is the saga of the Long Stagger. Compilers of the *Guinness Book of Records* kindly take note. It occurred in the Square of Listowel in the year nineteen fifty-eight. I cannot say for certain what the precise hour was but I recall clearly that it was the second night of the race week and that there was a tremendous crowd in town for the occasion.

Public houses were packed to capacity and the sounds of revelry could be heard afar. The streets were thronged and occasionally a drunkard would stagger from left to right and vice versa to the accompaniment of anxious screams from passing ladies who were not at all used to such Bacchanalian behaviour. After a few short, preliminary staggers the drunkards would gradually launch into longer staggers until they fell to the ground in some out-of-the-way place or were moved by the Civic Guards.

Those early, tentative staggers reminded me of the awkward attempts of fledglings as they flew uncertainly from perch to perch or from nest to ground until such time as they had mastered fairly long flights. Then, when they thought they had mastered the process, they would become reckless and fly with naked abandon until inevitably they came to grief.

So it was with the staggering drunkards. Having survived the first stagger they lurched and reeled from one side of the roadway to the other, missing pedestrians and traffic by fractions of inches until their confidence was such that they thought themselves immune to hurt. This overconfidence was their ruin. Soon they were to fall by the wayside. When sobriety returned the morning

13

after, the damage had been done. There would be strained muscles, fractured or broken limbs or worst of all, in the eyes of the beholder, serious facial disfiguration ranging from the simple thick lip to the broken nose to the more fetching black eye.

It should be said at this point that the Listowel Square stagger of nineteen fifty-eight resulted in no real injury, apart from a bump in the head, and this despite the fact that it was probably the most complete and elaborate stagger ever witnessed in that noted place of many staggers.

Because of space restrictions, I will name but a few of the many staggers which have evolved over the years. We have aided staggers, jaded staggers, group staggers, accidental staggers and staggered staggers. These are only staggers of a kind and, to fulfil a comprehensive stagger, the staggerer must move unaided from one area to another without damage to himself or to others and, in that comprehensive stagger, must complete the entire range of staggers great and small.

The onlooker who has not made a careful study of drunken staggers may be deceived easily by the running stagger. This dangerous, probably the most dangerous, form of stagger would come under the head of the aided stagger mentioned earlier. There are only two methods of indulging in the running stagger. The first and most common is to miss a step, be that step an exit or kerb-step or otherwise. The second method is to be in receipt of a push in the back whilst walking down a street with a fairly steep incline. In both cases the running staggerer is caught unawares and although his stagger is fast and bewilderingly tricky, it always ends in disaster. One way or another, and in no time at all, he ends up in a heap.

The man who completed the Marathon Stagger in Listowel's town Square was below average height. For all that, he was broadshouldered, firmly built and bowlegged. In short he was possessed of all the points of your classic staggerer. In addition he was drunk and this is the most important point of all because, whether we like it or not, there are few sober staggerers and the few who exist are more dodderers than they are staggerers. No one takes them seriously and nobody moves very far out of their way.

Different then was the small bowlegged man who erupted from the door of the Listowel Square public house on that faraway night to shatter all existing records. After erupting he burped loudly and swayed back and forth in an endeavour to take stock of his surroundings. His eyes were glazed and it was clear to be seen that he had no idea where he was nor, indeed, did he care where he was. With a resigned sigh which intimated that he had been in similar situations before he threw back his shoulders and lurched forward like a colt from a starting gate.

He went directly across the square in a straight line until he came to the railings of the Church of Ireland. He made no attempt to seize hold of the railings. Instead, without pausing for a second, he lurched backward and staggered in a clockwise fashion around the perimeter of the church.

I should proceed no further unless I state here that the backward stagger is the most precarious of all gymnastic movements. A fall can be fatal and often has been. Only genuine drunkards manage to survive such disasters. There is no psychological explanation for this. It is a fact of life.

Let us return to our friend and to that historic night in 1958. Our bowlegged but intrepid staggerer, having completed a half-circuit of the Protestant church, suddenly staggered sideways at a truly frightening rate in the general direction of the neighbouring Catholic church before staggering backwards again and completing his circuit of the Protestant church. It was as though the poor fellow was endeavouring to show that he was a man of tolerance as well as a man of action. When he completed the full circuit he continued without stopping or without looking until he disappeared through that very same public house door from which he first emerged.

It was the most remarkable feat I have ever seen. The man who was with me at the time was equally impressed. It was a colossal stagger and it was truly comprehensive. We followed him into the pub and saw him, still staggering in circles and half-circles until he turned once more and headed for the door.

All the time his eyes were either closed or partly closed. In the Square once more he moved towards Leahy's corner, staggering in all directions but still managing to maintain a true course. The corner almost proved to be too much for him. He negotiated it nevertheless. He then staggered across the road, spurning the heavy traffic until he came to Lynch's corner. From here he proceeded into William Street where he headed for the doorway of another public house. He staggered straight into the arms of a burly doorman who spun him around and dispatched him back the way he had come.

This was his downfall. While there could be no doubt that he was a past master of the natural stagger he could not cope with the aided stagger. After twenty paces he lurched across the roadway and was so tripped by the kerb that he managed to bang

15

his head against the stone front of a shop. He fell in a heap and, when we bent to aid him, we were greeted by a profound snore which seemed to suggest that he was sleeping the sleep of the just and I venture to suggest that no man in the town of Listowel was more entitled to that same sleep on that eventful night.

Will Regan Play the Fiddle?

My first attempt at writing for the theatre was a runaway success. The year was nineteen forty-three and a group of us, all under sixteen, decided to hold a concert in a disused and decaying shed at the top of the street. My incredible success came about quite by accident.

In our anxiety to present an appealing show we forgot about posters. I was immediately commissioned to do the needful. The star of our show was a youngster by the name of Will Regan. Will was an up and coming violinist and it was decided that he would top the bill. There were other candidates such as a lad who could eat a raw chop in a matter of seconds and another who could drink a full bottle of table sauce without ever taking the bottle from his head. We also had a belcher, i.e., a boy who could stand up before an audience and give an exhibition of belching ranging from staccato-like burps to long, froglike croaks. We decided, however, on Will Regan. We also decided on one poster. We felt that one big poster would have a greater impact than several small ones.

Across the top of the poster I intended to write in sprawling red capitals: "WILL REGAN WILL PLAY THE FIDDLE". In my hurry what I wrote was: "WILL REGAN PLAY THE FIDDLE".

Nobody noticed the mistake until the poster was on display in the town square. Did I come in for derision when the error was copped! I felt like leaving town for good. In despair I went to local painter Francie Chute and asked him if anything could be done to transform the poster. He came and had a critical look.

"My friend," said he, "do not attempt to tamper with this poster. It is a masterpiece. By the end of the week everybody in town will be asking the same question."

"What question?" I asked.

"Will Regan play the fiddle?" Francie replied without batting an eyelid.

How right he was. Not only was the question on the lips of everybody in the town of Listowel but it was being asked further afield in the hills and dales and boglands all around North Kerry.

Men and women took to stopping one another on the street and asking the same question: "Will Regan play the fiddle?"

We even received a telegram from a person unknown based in the city of Dublin. The telegram simply asked; "Will Regan play the fiddle?"

Soon word spread to the neighbouring town of Tralee and eventually to Killarney. In every pub and at every crossroads the question was being asked. My friend Francie Chute had recognised a masterpiece when he saw one. He went so far as to paint a banner, free of charge. We hung it between two telephone poles near the main entrance to the town. On it in a variety of colours in the inimitable Chute style was written the question: "WILL REGAN PLAY THE FIDDLE?"

There was only one way to find out and that was to go to the concert. Eventually the fateful afternoon came around. It was standing room only not to mention the fact that outside the hall a large crowd had also gathered.

Alas and alack there was no sign of Will Regan. Some said he had gone fishing. More said he had gone swimming. The pressure, unfortunately, had been too much for him. It became my painful duty to inform the capacity crowd that Will Regan would not play the fiddle, at least not then, at a later date definitely but not on the date advertised. There were catcalls and boos. Several called for their money but in the best tradition of the theatre the show went on regardless.

The years passed and occasionally in a public house or at a street corner a wag would ask, "Will Regan play the fiddle?"

No one dared answer because no one could be sure. They would keep asking the question nevertheless in the hope that one day it would be answered. It was probably the most successful line I ever wrote and to think that I wrote it unwittingly.

I remember a few years back to have a play opening in Dublin's Olympia Theatre. It was a wet night and as my wife and I wended our way across the slippery streets from the Ormond Hotel we heard a voice call out from the shadows of a side street.

"Will Regan play the fiddle?" came the haunting query.

When I looked there was nobody to be seen, not even a shadow.

Irish Nudism

The proposal that nudist beaches should be introduced into Ireland has been greeted, in the main, with shock and horror. Never mind the fact that every other country in Europe has espoused them. Never mind the fact that Adam and Eve went around without as much as a pair of socks or garters and never mind the fact that female nudity in ancient Ireland was looked upon as a blessed art form.

"Beannacht leat!" The blessing is as old as the hills and what it means simply is, "A naked woman to you!"

Then there's the couplet from the ancient Cork marching song:

The Blackpool girls are very rude,
They go swimming in the nude.

So why should the Ireland of today be so critical of nudism on isolated beaches? Surely if grown men and women wish to expose their pelts to the elements they should be allowed to do so, provided, of course, they do so out of sight of the general public.

I'll say one thing for Ireland and the Irish. We are consistent. The minute sex or nudity is mentioned there is absolute uproar while rape, mugging, bombing, shooting and arson are tolerated at what are euphemistically known as acceptable levels. Why, one is tempted to ask, should the bared female posterior, for instance, strike such fear and foreboding into the minds and hearts of so many corporations and county councils when terrorism and mayhem are taken for granted? What is it about the Irish that induces such delirium and hysteria at the prospect of innocent nudity?

I put the question to a female acquaintance in a neighbourhood hotel the other night. She pondered well before committing herself.

"I don't mind if they parade up and down these beaches naked or half-naked," said she, "so long as I don't have to do it, for," she finished with a whimper, "I can't stand any sort of cold."

Nobody I asked, in fact, had the slightest objection to nudist beaches so long as they were out of the way of children and religious.

"I don't know so much about nudist beaches," said Davy Gunn, the bodhrawn-maker, "but I mind we had nudist strands along the banks of the Smearla River when I was a gorsoon."

I expressed some suprise at this.

"Oh it was quite common," Davy Gunn assured me, "barring alone for those that had bathing togs or would use football togs."

"And were there many objections from corporation and county council members?" I asked.

"I never heard a word of objection," said Davy Gunn. "Man dear, it was a common thing for farmers' boys and farmers' sons and farmers themselves to canter down to the strand on the riverbank at the end of a hot day. Very seldom you'd see anyone with a bathing togs. You might bring the head of a brush and a knob of carbolic soap to scrub yourself but devil the more!"

"Would you have towels?" I asked.

Gunn laughed uproariously at this preposterous question.

"What would we want towels for and the meadows in bloom! You could roll over and over like a donkey till you were dry or you could go for a canter along one of the inches till you were dried by the wind."

"You're sure there was no bathing togs?"

"I never saw a pair in those days. If 'twas to Ballybunion now or to Ballyheigue you were going to you might carry a football togs but there was nothing only the bare pelt along the strands of the Smearla River."

"And none thought it wrong?"

"How could it be wrong? Aren't our skins our own? Man dear, it was considered a fine thing. You see there were no bathrooms in those days. Anyway, if a man can go bare into a bath to clean himself why shouldn't he be able to go bare into a river to clean himself? Another thing is that you couldn't wash all of yourself with togs on but in the bare pelt you could scrub every corner."

All of this, of course, still leaves us with the vexing question as to why council members and corporation members should be so opposed to nudism.

The Frying Pan Incident

I will call this tale the Frying Pan Incident. I might have calefacted another, more attractive title but I think my choice will be vindicated at the end of an authentic story which deals with human indifference and the reactions which it provokes. It all happened a long time ago but not until recently has the second of the two principals involved departed the scene. The first surrendered his spirit to his maker after a drunken outing at a Listowel horse fair. The other, his spouse, disintegrated one evening after she received a fright from a bull. Now that they are both safely dispatched to their eternal rewards I may begin.

I beheld them on that fateful September night so many moons ago as they paused by my door on their way to the amusements centre in the market place. He walked in front, head held high, chin jutting upward and outward, she behind in sole command of five obstreperous brats, four of them boys, one a girl.

They crossed to Market Street outside my very door. This afforded me the most intimate of views. When they had crossed he raised his left hand without looking behind him and indicated to his long-suffering wife with slanted thumb that she was to proceed with her wayward clutch to the scene of the amusements. With that gesture he abdicated all responsibility for the care of his children. Without a word he entered a pub. I remembered him from somewhere but memory failed to accommodate me. Later in the night it all came back.

It was in Ballybunion on the fifteenth of August, the day of the annual pattern. It was the hat I recalled. It was either the same as the one he presently wore or he had purchased a similar type recently. I saw him with his hand around the slender waist of a lovely girl who happened to be wearing a white frock. She was now the mother of his children but she had deteriorated more than somewhat in the intervening years.

They were walking along the beach and he held her tight lest she fall into the ocean or be carried away by a whale maybe. They were not married then and many onlookers, myself included, remarked how attached the young man was to the girl in the white frock, whose face had been kissed by the summer sun and whose eyes shone as stars shine when the heavens are clear.

Later still I saw them in the village proper. They were eating ice cream cones. He clutched her hand fearing she might fall over a concealed pebble or be thrown onto the roadway by a heedless pedestrian. He seemed truly determined that she should come to no harm. It was clear to be seen that he was prepared to lay down his life in her defence although it was difficult to see from where danger threatened. Still, I suppose, better be sure than sorry.

I came across them for the third and final time that night in a popular hostelry which I had entered in search of diversion with a party of friends. Again there was the sheltering arm, this time around her shoulders. It guarded her from unseen dangers and was a guarantee too that she would not fall from the chair on which she so demurely sat. In his hand he held a partially consumed pint of stout whilst underneath his chair stood another pint, this one full. It was full, in fact, as the tide which was waxing to its ultimate on the nearby golden sands beneath the glinting cliffs of Doon. His eyes, let me add, were bloodshot and bleary and it seemed he must have his way with the unfortunate girl before the night ran its course.

I saw them many a time after but never again, not even one single time, did I see him with his arm around her or his hand holding hers. Cynics may say that this is the way of the world but this is not so at all for people may hold hands forever if a little love remains.

Others might suggest that she had matured so much in the interim she no longer needed anybody to save her from falling over the likes of an empty chip carton or a discarded matchbox. I'm afraid that the nub of the trouble was that he always put himself first, that he considered himself to be the most important person in the whole wide world, that his wife was a chattel, an encumbrance and the children nuisances to be tolerated day in, day out.

I had seen them quite a lot in recent times, she struggling under the weight of two heavy grocery bags whilst he, like a gamecock, strutted towards his car. There was always an uncaring smile on his sideburned face, a feather in his undersized hat and the inevitable, telltale porter stains at the corners of his mouth.

I watched her now as she endeavoured to guide her flock across the dangerous roadway, a roadway filled with cars whose drivers never consider women and children waiting to cross from one side to the other. The exercise extended her to the utmost. Fatigued, she leaned against a wall at the far side but the uncontrollable children, with no father's hand to restrain them, gave her no respite. She followed one here, another there, cautioned one and threatened one. Eventually she managed to corral them but there was no telling when one or all would break loose again.

The night went by. People passed to and fro in carnival or in drunken mood. Then at the call of time the public houses began to disgorge their hundreds of customers. Wife and children, huddled under an awning, waited patiently for himself to appear. I was, alas, not a witness to the subsequent proceedings but fortunately for me a reliable friend was. He was then a member of the Garda Síochána and it was he who later filled me in.

The woman and her five children had a long wait before our man eventually emerged from the public house where he had been guzzling beyond his means. He had warned them to wait no matter what and he had threatened torture and beatings if they dared to be a moment late. He was the very last man to leave the licensed premises in question. He looked up and down and hither and thither when the pub door was closed behind him. He pretended he did not see his long-suffering wife and children a few yards away.

His wife, pathetic little creature, saw to her flock and prepared to follow in her master's uneven wake but then a fight broke out between the four boys. She found herself unable to stop them. In vain she called upon her husband to intervene but he ignored her by the simple expedient of turning his head as though nothing was happening. She called him again and again but he pretended he did not hear. It would never do if a man with such a fine feather on such a jaunty hat were to be associated with this motley collection of urchins.

He walked away and left his poor wife to cope alone. Then the unexpected happened. It often does when a woman is pushed too far. She happened at the time to be carrying a frying pan which she had won in a lottery in the amusements arcade. Without as much as a word she ran after him and whacked him on the side of the head with the body of the pan. It was not the first time a harrassed wife resorted to the frying pan, mighty feller of unresponsive spouses.

The next time I saw him he had a bandage around his head but he also had a child by the hand and another in his arms.

Owl Sandwiches

It was a warm day during the most recent summer. The time was four thirty of a Monday afternoon. Normally I would be closed since Monday is the official half-day in Listowel. However, I had been alerted that some tourists were on the way so I elected to remain open. The bar was all but deserted. There were two middle-aged, sunburned female refugees from the nearby seaside resort of Ballybunion and two coffee-drinking nuns. The only other person present was the inimitable Davy Gunn, bodhrawn-maker extraordinary, raconteur, historian and dairy farmer. A brace of house flies buzzed the drowsy inmates while the beer cooler could be heard droning loudly, such was the general silence of the place.

"What manner of sandwiches are them there?" Davy Gunn asked as he indicated a towering dish of unsold collations displayed on a shelf behind the counter.

"Chicken, mutton and beef," I responded with alacrity. The sandwiches, plump and beautiful, had been on view since opening time without attracting a solitary offer.

"Give me a chicken sandwich," said Gunn, "and see could you banish the daylight from this empty glass."

I refilled his glass and selected a chicken sandwich. Not a word from the other occupants of the bar although they never took their eyes off Gunn or myself during our transactions. This is a trying time in a public house. Customers, particularly strange ones, tend to be silent and over-observant. In the absence of crowds and bustle or other diversions they are transformed into scrutineers. They are waiting for something to happen, for somebody else to perform. They preserve the divine right of non-participation and subscribe nothing to the progress of the day.

Then as expected the door swings open and a large party of colourfully dressed Continentals enter. They seem glum enough too. They look here, there and everywhere without uttering a word.

Meanwhile Davy Gunn is busily masticating his sandwich with an air of sublime contentment. All his attention is directed to the consumption of this modest lunch. The Continentals observe his every mastication as though he were on display. Then for the first time mutterings, natterings and diverse grunts are exchanged. The outpourings are Germanic in sound. The party numbers fourteen and soon all are conversing excitedly. There are five males and nine females. No doubt they are part of a tour, the others probably having opted for drinks or coffees in the nearby hotel.

One of the party, a well-rounded female with a homely face, approaches Davy Gunn and asks if sandwiches are available. Gunn surveys the woman quizzically for a moment or two and then nods politely. He cannot speak because his mouth is filled with bread and chicken. However, this powerful female goes one further and asks him what kind of sandwiches are to be had.

"Houl'," Gunn answers, and then to the nuns, "Don't they know a man isn't supposed to talk with his mouth full."

"Vat did he say?" the other members of the tour ask the well-rounded spokesperson.

"Der sandviches sim to be owl sandviches," she informs them. Gunn laughs loud and long at the thought of owl sandwiches but he pats his tummy nevertheless and intimates by a series of emphatic ums and mums that the sandwiches are highly palatable.

Some of the visitors crinkle up their faces at the thought of owl sandwiches but the remainder express delight and surprise. Soon most of them are happily munching owl sandwiches.

"Iss werry lak chicken," an elderly man confides as he launches into his second bite.

"Nein, nein," says his companion, "iss better to chicken. Dis owl sandvich hass a real flavour lak owl."

Drinks are ordered, pints and half pints of lager. It is turning into a festive occasion. Even the nuns are smiling.

"Show me out them beef and mutton sandwiches," Davy Gunn directs and then with a dish held aloft he addresses those who had turned up their noses at the owl sandwiches.

"Duck sandwiches!" he calls out, "gander sandwiches!"

Soon there wasn't a single, solitary sandwich left in the dish. The Continentals, male and female, displayed an astonishing capacity for consuming larger. Eventually the driver of the tour bus had to come looking for them. He was most annoyed. He was addressed by the female who had first spoken to Davy Gunn.

"You should haff yourself an owl sandvich," she told him, "it make you feel better."

Corner Boys 1

Regular readers who have noted my many observations on corner boys sometimes ask me if the corner boys ever resent what I write about them.

"I mean," a reader said to me recently, "you often mention that you can see them from your window. They know that they are the corner boys you're writing about. If it was me I wouldn't like it because I think what you write is provocative. In fact I think I would probably send you a solicitor's letter."

I told him I was glad he brought up the subject. The truth is that of all the corner boys ever described only one showed any signs of resentment. The others seem not to care and, in fact, one approached me recently of a Sunday morning and shook hands with me complimenting me on my powers of sagacity and perception.

The mother of another told me that her son had given up being a corner boy after reading about himself in one of my essays. I was sorry to hear this because he was a dedicated corner boy and a great source of inspiration to me personally. He abandoned cornering altogether and found gainful employment in a local factory. He is now a part-time corner boy but the professional touch is missing.

Anyway enough of that. Let us refer now to that solitary corner boy who resented my writing about him and his equals. My first indication of his displeasure came one night in the middle of a pub quiz. My team were playing an away game and the venue was crowded. There I was with the rest of the onlookers vainly racking my brains for the answer to a difficult eight-marker. The question had been, what great event took place in Clare on the twenty-fourth of June? Nobody knew the answer. The answer of course was the fair of Spancel Hill. The clue lies in the lines "It was on the twenty-third of June, the day before the fair."

Anyway upon lifting my glass with a view to swallowing some of its contents I got a fairly solid thump on the back. When I turned round I found myself confronted with an extremely drunken and hostile face.

"What's the idea?" I asked.

"Think you're smart, don't you?" said the man who had delivered the thump. His eyes were bloodshot, his teeth were bared and there was a snarl to him. A lesser man than myself might have quailed.

"What's up?" I asked. Ordinarily I would ignore such a thump but the fellow had made me spill the greater part of my pint.

Now the Keanes are normally a reasonable bunch although quick to anger when grievously wronged. They'll not look for trouble but they won't lie down either. You might kick a Keane on the shin without fear of physical retaliation. You may even stand on his corns or obscure his view at a football game but there is one thing you must never do and that is spill his drink. The Keanes are pernickety in this respect.

When I pointed out to the offender that he had indeed spilled my drink he responded that he would just as soon spill my blood.

"You're a great fellow writing about corner boys," he said and again he ground his teeth. It was only then I remembered that I had indeed written about him. What I had written was not in the least derogatory. It was the way he interpreted it or even worse he probably heard it second hand from a mischief-maker who distorted it.

"Now my friend," I informed him, "let there be no more thumping."

"I am not your friend," he stormed.

"Quiet please!" The injunction came from the quiz master. There the argument ended. As I said he was the only corner boy that I know of who resented my writing about him.

He still frequents corners and occasionally he looks up at my window as if he were daring me to come down and face him on his own terrain.

I will concede that he is a first-rate corner boy. He never

intimidates dawdlers and trespassers or obstructs passers-by. He never answers people who seek directions. He disappears at the first sign of trouble. He looks into space all day long and, generally speaking, does all that is required of a typical corner boy. Aspiring corner boys please note.

"The Suckund Woige"

"A Wodka and fite," said the countryman, "and a small fuishkey."

His request drew titters from the barmaid who recognised him for what he was, a small farmer who spoke the English of his fathers who, in turn, spoke an English which sounded very like the Irish language of their fathers. Nothing to be ashamed of although it is understandable why it evoked the titters.

Your true West-Munster man has always scorned the letter V and not just because there is no V in the Irish alphabet. It does not complement his Irish-indebted articulation and it impedes his natural flow of speech.

I remember at the National School there was a gorsoon from the north of the town who could not pronounce the word "very". He pronounced it "wery" just as Sam Weller did in *Pickwick Papers*. "Wery well," he would say to the teacher who enunciated the word carefully and repeatedly and told the gorsoon to practice it at home. In this case practice did not make perfect. The teacher wisely gave up and allowed the youngster to stick to the language of his fathers.

In Bawn's public house in Dingle only last year I listened to as lovely and beautifully distorted a piece of mispronunciation as ever dropped from the lips of a West Kerryman.

"Wentry hawe a lowely wiew," said he after I told him that we had been visiting that part of the peninsula before stopping off at Paddy Bawn's for some refreshments.

"What did he say?" The question came from a female member of our party.

27

"He said, 'Ventry has a lovely view,'" I informed her.

"No he didn't," she said. When I explained that he used the letter W instead of V she attempted in vain to mouth the same descriptive sentence. Although she was a teacher with some knowledge of elocution she failed lamentably and spent the remainder of the day trying to master the rich and uniquely sounding description of Ventry.

At the heel of the evening she was making no better a fist of it than when she was after first hearing it. Weeks were to pass before she would master it. If there is any reader linguistically inclined let him or her endeavour to reel it off without first practising its rolling nuances and see how far they'll succeed. It's worth trying, however, as an exercise in acceptable mispronunciation, acceptable for the good reason that it is part and parcel of our heritage.

"Will you sample a drink?" I asked the man who lauded Ventry.

"Foi nat I" said he and he emptied his glass lest I change my mind.

"What did he say?" asked the teacher.

"Fot did she say?" asked the West Kerryman.

"She wanted to know what did you say," I informed him.

"Oh!" said he, "she's from the city is she?"

"What did he say?" the teacher repeated her question, "after you asked him to have the drink?"

"He said, 'Why not I?'" I told her.

"No," she argued, "he said, 'Foi nat I?'"

"Same thing," I told her as I opened a conversation in Irish with the West Kerryman. Here he was on absolutely safe ground, confident and elegant, distinct and accentual. We listened in wonder as he outlined a list of local beauty spots worth a visit. I translated for the others as best I could while he enunciated at breakneck speed. A native Irish speaker from West Kerry who is fully primed with strong drink is a hard man to follow unless you happen to be another West Kerryman.

We left the pub enlightened, also well-versed in local lore and related topography.

When the barmaid tittered at the man who called for "wodka and fite" she was doing him something of an injustice. In Russia wodka is also called by its correct name of wodka so that our friend was at least half right even if he did say fite.

"When I'm in town," I once heard the great and late Dan Paddy Andy O'Sullivan say, "I talks slow so that townies can understand me but fwen I'm away fon the town I talks away as I plaise."

Near the village of Ballyduff between Ballybunion and Tralee there is a lovely strand called Kilmore. One fine summer's day several years ago I happened to be strolling along a dune which afforded an excellent view of the Feale River which emptied itself into the sea just below me. All of a sudden a man appeared from the Ballyduff direction. He wore a cap on the side of his head and as he walked he staggered all over the place. It looked as if he must fall into the water at any minute. Miraculously he preserved his balance and as he drew near I noted a glazed look in his eyes.

I could not decide whether he was suffering from some serious physical disability or was just plain drunk. There was simply no way of telling from where I watched. I was joined by a native of the place who happened to be a cousin of mine and a great fellow for country talk with its lovely, native flavour and beautiful nuances. As we took in the progress of the man on the beach that worthy collapsed in a heap without as much as a moan. I was about to rush to the unfortunate man's aid when the cousin laid a restraining hand upon my elbow.

"Fot ails you?" he asked.

"That man seems to have suffered a heart attack," I told him.

"That man," said he in the peerless patois of the place, "is arter the suckund woige to the willage."

At first I was somewhat stymied but then I pondered long and well on what he had said.

"That man is arter the suckund woige to the willage".

It simply meant that he was after the second voyage to the village, the village in question being Ballyduff. We, therefore, must deduce as follows: during the first of his voyages to the village he got drunk. Then he returned home where we may safely conclude that he had a sleep and a bit to eat. Then he set out on the second voyage to the village. During this voyage, or rather upon his arrival in Ballyduff, he got drunk a second time. By the time he reached Kilmore Strand he was befuddled and exhausted and unable to complete the journey to his home which was still a good half mile away.

Drunk and fatigued he threw himself down on the warm sand and fell asleep instantly. I'm sorry it should have taken so long to translate a single sentence. It has taken me several whereas it only took my cousin one. Of course he had the advantage of local knowledge but, nevertheless, I feel that nobody could put it better than he did. Nowadays whenever I see a drunken man and that's rare enough, God knows, I simply say to myself that he's arter the suckund woige to the willage.

I'd need a wodka and fite after all that although on second thoughts I think that a small fuishkey would be better.

Aspiring politicians would be well advised to acquaint themselves with local accents and distortions of pronounciation. A man with a strange accent has no business asking the number one from a man who speaks the tongue of his fathers.

A Listowel Mutton Pie

The Listowel mutton pie is famed the world over and rightly so. It is a durable and palatable piece of pastry and holds fresh, without concession to rot, for several weeks. When served after being allowed to simmer in mutton broth it is absolutely delicious.

The following story concerning its inveteracy is a true one. During the first year of the second World War a young gentleman from the city of Limerick spent his holidays in the town of Listowel for the duration of the week of the races.

"Apart from booze," he confided to me years later, "my main diet was mutton pies served in mutton soup. But for those pies and that soup I would have succumbed to the shakes and wound up in a sanatorium."

After a most enjoyable week in Listowel he spent the first half of his final day in bed. He rose for late mass and partook of no drink that night.

The following Monday morning he knelt beside his bed and said his prayers. When he came downstairs he informed his father and mother that he feared for the safety of his city and his country and that he was off to enlist in the Irish navy. The year was nineteen forty-three.

The name of the ship on which he served as an able-bodied seaman is not known to me but it was a ship of the Muirchu which was the name of our navy in those distant days and a jolly and a courageous navy it was to be sure.

Time passed and our young friend became somewhat accustomed to the vagaries of the rude Atlantic. Nobody ever becomes accustomed fully to this vast and unpredictable body of water. Eventually he found himself one wintry evening acting as lookout. No pair of eyes ever scanned a sea so dutifully. Every other minute he blew his breath upon the lenses of his binoculars and shone them with a piece of chamois concealed underneath his cap.

At the time the ship was on mine-sweeping duties. Vigilance was essential if the corvette was not to be blown to pieces. Then suddenly the hair stood like boar bristles on the head of our look-out. He polished his lenses and looked a second time.

He could not be certain. There was some sort of strange object several hundred yards off the port bow, impossible to identify, but all objects were of immense significance at that time and in that place. Was it a mine or was it part of a sub? He decided to notify the skipper who, with the aid of a powerful telescope, examined the object at length. The skipper then handed over to his first officer who also made a thorough examination. The rest of the crew indulged in their own scrutinies but at the end of the survey each and every man aboard confessed to being totally confounded, bewildered and perplexed.

They had never seen a similar object before nor any object which even remotely resembled the one which now drifted off the port bow.

The captain was a fine sober type of officer not given to making hasty decisions or endangering his crew and vessel. He decided to venture no nearer the object. For three days and three nights he shadowed it. It drifted steadily south by southwest at a speed of five knots.

Finally upon sighting some trawlers in the distance he decided the time for action had come. The trawlers would have been returning home to Dingle and Cahersiveen and he feared for their safety. He, therefore, alerted his gun crews and told them to prepare for action.

He bided his time till the trawlers sailed outside his line of fire. Then he gave the order. Salvo after salvo was directed at the mysterious craft but no dent whatsoever did the constant barrage make upon it. It drifted unchanging as though it had been pelted by a shower of pebbles. However, I think it would only be fair if we were to allow the Limerick sailor, also a bit of a poet to take over here:

By Cahersiveen while patrolling

We sighted this strange-lookin' yoke,
"Open fire 'tis a mine," roared our skipper
Then our four inch and two inches spoke.
We fired till the guns nearly melted
Then the skipper called, "Look-out! What's nigh?"
"I'm blowed," said that worthy in tones far from sturdy,
"If it ain't a Listowel mutton pie!"

Anyway, to conclude, the pie was brought aboard without a mark on it, taken to the galley, allowed to simmer in some freshly made mutton broth and presented to the skipper who declared that he had never eaten anything half as nice before. I'll say no more. *Facile est inventis addere.*

Marital Storms

It is with some reluctance that I assume the role of marriage counsellor. Recently at a wedding I was, unexpectedly, called upon to say a few words on behalf of the bride's side of the house. Her father, articulate at fair and mart, refused to say anything on the grounds that whenever he rose to speak in public he was immediately struck dumb.

Most of those present had heard me hold forth before and so were familiar with all my hoary matrimonial anecdotes. I was almost at a loss for words when my wife thrust a glass of whiskey into my hand. Fortified by a hearty swallow I held forth for a short while and while I did not exactly cover myself with glory I did manage to evoke a few titters from the females and one or two inebriated guffaws from the men.

I sat down, greatly relieved to have, as it were, escaped with a caution. The moral here is that it is a foolish relative who goes to a wedding feast without a few words up his sleeve.

An aspect of marriage which is always overlooked by men desperate for anecdotes is disharmony. Love, of course, is the *sine qua non* of all marriages but the common or garden row is almost as important.

A marriage without a row is like an apple pie without cloves. However, I would not condone the banging of doors during rows. Neither would I approve of the breaking of crockery. Doors must be repaired and crockery must be replaced and these things cost money. The type of row I have in mind is the all-out verbal confrontation where no holds are barred, where nothing is held back, where old sores are reopened. A row of such proportions is almost as good as a general confession.

Great benefits accrue from such a row. In the first place the air is cleared. Secondly there will be no likelihood of another row for months afterwards. Thirdly the antagonists are so exhausted afterwards that all they are fit for is falling into each other's arms for support.

Those married couples who engage in such rows should never take eavesdroppers or neighbours into consideration. Otherwise the row might well be minimised and thus rendered useless as a cure for marital ailments. Even children should not be taken into consideration. I know that it can be hurtful to children to hear their parents shouting at each other but children soon learn that the occasional row is part and parcel of the home environment and is nothing to be ashamed of regardless of its dimensions. They will learn from an early age that rows pass quickly and that afterwards there will be harmony. Some children slip quietly out of the house but others prefer to remain knowing that nothing but good can come from the exchanges.

Embarrassment or any sense of shame should never be felt by either the offspring or the participants. The occasional row is part and parcel of married life and must never be seen as a defect in the marriage. Under no circumstances must there be an apology on its behalf because without regular rows marriages might well fall apart. Drunken rows, however, can be disastrous and if either or both of the partners are in the least spifflicated the row is nothing more than a drunken shambles, debasing and disgraceful, unworthy of the partners in such a great and noble contract.

I concede that there have been successful marriages without resorting to rows but these are few and far between and cannot have been very exciting to begin with.

Most marital eruptions are caused by stress, strain, lack of funding, impatience and intolerance. Like all storms there are numerous warning signs. Some irresponsible husbands pull up stakes at these signs and so deprive their wives of a chance to unleash their pent-up grievances. Most husbands stick to their guns as do most wives. Some, while they suffer throughout its duration, regard it as a sort of spring cleaning of the marriage stakes.

If the row does not hurt and shatter it has not fulfilled its purpose. It can, in fact, do more harm than good. My advice is let it rip. "Cry havoc and let slip the dogs of war," as Shakespeare said.

Any attempts by outsiders to come between the warring pair should not be tolerated. All a really good marital row needs is two people. Three's really a crowd in such a climate.

Running for cover to the homes of relations or sympathisers is also out of the question. The durability of marriage is forged from great verbal confrontations where the sky is the limit as far as invective and slagging are concerned.

From a purely personal point of view I can assure readers that a good row often shakes up a lackadaisical marital relationship and indeed has often saved a teetering marriage from toppling over the brink.

Sayings of the Week

At the end of each week we are treated in certain newspapers to the more memorable sayings of the week in question. To tell the truth, however, I cannot recall a single one of these choice pronouncements offhand. Could it be that we will never again see the equals of Wilde or Shaw or could it be that we are selecting the sayings of the wrong people?

Shortly before he died Oscar Wilde called for champagne and when it was brought declared: "I am dying, as I have lived, beyond my means."

Now there's a quality quip. Asked about religion Shaw had this to say: "There's only one religion although there are hundreds of versions of it." Shaw had the knack.

The quotes we read every week come not from the common man but from bishops and ministers, business moguls and trade union leaders, writers and academics. All worth hearing from I'm sure but they are hindered by knowledge and caution and must perforce lack the rude and ready wit of the man on the street.

One wet day Davy Gunn, the bodhrawn-maker, was confronted by an itinerant for the third time. The fellow had a hangover and requested the price of another drink from Gunn who had already come to his aid earlier in the day.

"Don't you know," said Gunn, "that beggars can't be boozers." Economic and to the point and worth inclusion in memorable sayings of the week.

On the same evening I attended a football game in the nearby town of Tarbert with a neighbour, Jerome Murphy. Towards the end of the game a free was granted to the losing side. The free went wide and as it did the kicker bent to see what was wrong with his shooting boot.

"A good free-kicker," said Jerome, "looks to his boot before he kicks the ball, not after."

Sound advice and worth inclusion for its sagacity alone.

In a local hostelry after the game a man was talking about a deaf priest in a contiguous parish. "All you have to do," said this recently and questionably shrived soul, "is talk reasonably loud to him. So long as he hears any kind of a murmur he's satisfied and there's no bother about the absolution."

"The bother with a deaf priest," said the man behind the counter, "is that while you may not be heard inside the box you'll certainly be heard outside it."

In the same bar later in the night a drunken malingerer with the vile habit of falling irrevocably asleep after one drink asked to be served. He was quietly but firmly refused .

"I can call for a drink in any pub in Ireland except this dive," he flung out.

"It's no bother call," said the man behind the counter; "getting served is your problem."

In my own pub one Sunday night I was introduced to a visitor from that hilly and lovely area between Abbeyfeale and Knocknagoshel.

"This is Keane, the playwright," said the man who performed the introduction.

"Playwrights," said the hillman, "only puts down what we says and charges us to hear it!"

Now there's a truth if ever there was one. And in the same bar I heard one man say to another, upon hearing that the other's son was in love and wanted to marry, "Love isn't something you find in the street. You must invest daily if you want it to mature."

The speaker was an insurance agent but what he had to say is worth considering before discarding. At least that would be my policy.

Now I will be the first to concede that not all the foregoing are out of the top drawer but some are and they are worth remembering. The man in the street represents the vast majority and deserves to be heard now and then. He doesn't need great occasions or horrible disasters to trigger him off. He works from the commonplace and he works off the cuff.

Afternoons

When I was a gorsoon in the Stacks Mountains there was no such an article as an afternoon. People had heard about it all right and were aware that afternoons went on elsewhere but they had no place in the lives of the people in the Stacks.

There were nights and days and evenings and now and then one would hear mention of twilight from the likes of school-masters and from those who were romantically inclined, but in all the time I sojourned in that part of the world there was never any mention of afternoons. I daresay it was because the early part was incorporated into day and the later part into evening.

In the town of Listowel it was somewhat different. The word afternoon was to be heard occasionally if one listened carefully or if one moved in the right circles. At that time in the town there were several practising Protestants and these were not above referring to that time between day and evening as afternoon. Nuns in the local convent and a few teachers would use the word afternoon on a regular basis but it never caught on in the outside world. I doubt, in fact, if it was meant to catch on.

Visitors from England and America nearly always used the

word afternoon and one sometimes heard mention of afternoon tea where we had no doubt the very best of china was used and where cucumber sandwiches, muffins and scones were nibbled by the upper crust.

There was no afternoon tea as such in the Stacks Mountains. There was a ritual known as the "evening tay" but this was mostly confined to areas such as the meadow and the bog. This "evening tay" was taken between half past three and four and was known amongst county council workers and other workers out on hire as the four o'clock tay.

The four o'clock tay was, in fact, at the centre of every bargain made between labourer and employer. The labourer would be told that he could expect his dinner in the middle of the day which was anytime between twelve and one o'clock and that he would receive his supper in the evening which meant anytime between six and seven.

The hassle began when the evening tay was suggested by the employee. Strictly speaking it meant that the recipient was entitled to a mug or cup of tea around four o'clock in the afternoon but there was a certain amount of small print and while the would-be employee, generally a farmer's labourer, never said so in so many words he would be expecting a slice of homemade currant cake or even a bun as well as the tea. The very least he felt he was entitled to was a slice or two of bread and jam. When a farmer capitulated too easily it often meant that the supper would not be up to the normal standard. That there might be no egg, only plain bread and tea.

Lunch was another word which was never mentioned. Like the afternoon it was around somewhere but it played no role in the life of the people of the Stacks. You got lunch in cities and in hotels but never in the countryside. The midday meal in rural Ireland was referred to as the dinner. It was the main meal of the day and it still is although more and more people refer to it as lunch but, of course, these would be having a second dinner in the evening.

"A good dinner is everything," country people would say. What they meant was that it would sustain a working man until the evening when his day's work ended. Evening dinner was invented by those who did not work. It is well known that people who do not work eat more than those who work hard.

This could very well be the reason why evening dinner replaced modest suppers. Any fool will tell you that a hotel lunch is the equivalent of a full dinner. Therefore, those who do not work eat two dinners in the same day. They need this second dinner to keep going until bedtime.

If evening dinner becomes a reality in every rural home it will mean that Irish country people will be sitting down to two dinners in any given day. This is how the decline and fall of ancient Rome started so those of you who have already commenced with this wilful practice cannot say you have not been warned.

Darling of the Spring

This very spring I almost despaired of ever hearing the cuckoo again. Without fail he has been arriving at the green groves of Affoulia next door to Dirha Bog which is next door to Listowel since bird migration first began. Always before the end of April he announces his arrival in his own inimitable fashion.

As soon as I arrive in the boglands I stand stock still and blow my nose, these antics being highly conducive to the sharpening of one's hearing. As I am mobilising my acoustics who should I notice overhead but a prime sparrow-hawk and he in an almighty hurry. For all his bravado by day he is very much afraid of the dark and likes to have the sheets drawn over his head before night descends.

I move onwards towards the cuckoo-Mecca of Affoulia and now a hunting barn owl wings low out of the distance resuming the everlasting hunt and replacing the hawk whose murderous vigil ends with the setting sun. The long, slim wings of the owl convey him with deadly silence from sally grove to copsewood, from dun-dark reek to turfbank, from cutaway to bogpool. I note his outsize head, his heart-shaped face, his underside of brown and yellow. He sees me and drifts effortlessly to where darkening shadows conceal him from prey and intruder alike.

Still no word from the cuckoo. A man pushing a bicycle on which are perched precariously two sacks of turf approaches and asks me for the time. I tell him I never carry a timepiece and I can see that he is not in the least bit thankful.

"You didn't by any chance hear the cuckoo?" I ask.

"There isn't much troubling you," he scoffs and wheels his precious, hard-won cargo over the bumpy bog road. Cuckoos have no place in this man's world. Neither have owls or sparrow-hawks or the hoarse-clocking hen pheasant who announces her availability to any and all cocks in the vicinity.

There is now a red glow where the cap of the sunken sun sat so brilliantly and so recently. Shortly now darkness will impose itself sombrely over the dusk and none of the sky's tenants save the owl and bat will venture abroad.

Still no sound from the groves of Affoulia. What if he doesn't come! A summer without a cuckoo would be like a breaker without spume, a duck without a quack, a harp without strings. My ears are cocked but there is nothing to be heard save the whispering of late April breezes in the scantily clad boughs of alder and sally. I begin to despair and, reluctantly, because darkness is nigh I retrace my steps to where I left my car. As I walk beneath a brightening moon I recall Wordsworth's lovely lines:

> Thrice welcome darling of the Spring!
> Even yet thou art to me
> No bird but an invisible thing,
> A voice, a mystery.

As I walk along the springy bog path chuckling waters accompany me. Gentle breezes apart these are the only sounds of the bogland. Then suddenly comes the faint and distant announcement from the balmy groves of Affoulia. It is certainly himself. There is no mistaking the traditional notes, the unique timbre, the absolute restraint and then the triumph as the announcement is repeated. The call comes near but fades again within his diminishing circles as he locates lodgings for the night.

Three more times he calls with emphasis.

"Cuckoo!" he calls which means, "I am come."

"Cuckoo!" he calls secondly which means, "Let there be sunshine from tomorrow forth."

"Cuckoo!" he finally calls which means, "Get out the slean. There's turf to be cut."

He does not mind that the members of the Listowel Urban Council have not come to welcome him. For him virtue is its own reward and it does not matter that no delegation of local farmers is waiting to greet him or that the priests of the surrounding parishes are not present to chant his praises in ringing Latin.

No bird of the air has ever spoken so economically and harmoniously of greenery's advent. He also implies that we may now forego our longjohns, place broom and laurel in the grate, replace our diminishing stocks of salad cream and generally gird ourselves for summer days.

Hail

I have heard of giant hailstones and jagged hailstones but these are peculiar only to far-off climes and we need not concern ourselves with them here. For instance I have never heard of anybody suffering death or serious injury as a result of having been struck by a hailstone. One may slip on a carpet of hailstones or one's car may skid but this is not really the fault of the hailstone any more than falling into a river is the fault of the river.

Indeed there has been more exaggeration with regard to hailstones than sleet, snow and ordinary raindrops put together. In the more whopping tales of travellers there have been mentions of hailstones as large as men's heads, veritable turnips of hail if we can believe such extravagant accounts.

Two of my favourite subjects are cuckoos and hailstones. You could say I suppose that they are both visitors from extremities: the cuckoo from the sunny lands of North Africa and the hailstone from the regions of ice. Not quite poles apart you might say but near enough.

Every year I eagerly await the arrivals of cuckoo and hail and I was delighted when I encountered my first decent shower of hailstones whilst walking through the boglands of Dirha this winter. Fair play to nature: she always sets the scene with the care and skill of the truly great artist that she is.

Before a single stone fell the signs of the impending onslaught were all around in the great body of the sky. Overhead were the pale patches of deceptive blue but advancing inexorably under the power of the east wind was a mighty rampart of menacing cloud, livid in hue, then puce and inky as the declining sun imposed its will on the colour scheme of the sky.

First came a single stone although stone, I think, is hardly the appropriate word. Gem or pearl would be far more apposite. First came a single pearl which tapped me gently on the forehead before melting into a celestial tear. It was nature's way of informing me that winter in all its fury had really come. Here was an accredited ambassador from its court.

Then came the daunting shower, the hail beating on the roadway and dancing thereon like beads of white marble. It made little sound and no sound at all as it landed on the rust-brown bog and lay on stems and blades and sprays, on whin, fern and bracken as though deliberately exhibiting itself to its utmost. Then, suddenly it stopped. Nothing passes as quickly as a shower of hail. Sleet cloys and sogs and generally outstays its welcome. Rain goes on and on and snow, for all its beauty, may well fall for tedious days on end but hail, hopping and happy, stays but a while.

It seems to reserve its more vigorous offensives, however, for corrugated iron roofs, fanlights and plate glass windows. On these its bombardments are noisy as kettle drums and frenetic as hornets but mercifully shortlived as the dramatic flight of a falling star or the frighful flash of lightning. To those who are familiar with its bluster and fury its arrival is to be savoured for what it is, simply a curt message from winter which states with emphasis that people without umbrellas, hats, overcoats and overshoes had better be on the look-out from now on. This is where the true suggestive power of the hailstone is manifested and this is why it is so well loved by the proprietors of draperies, shoe shops and fuel depots. There is no need for them to advertise their wares. Every hailstone that harrasses the human and the human habitation is an advertisement in itself. When it beats upon window or rooftop nothing so forcibly reminds those who hear its inimitable exordium that their toes are soon likely to be cold.

Of course, hail without frost dies instantly and for all its beauty leaves behind no more than a flood at best but better, many will agree, a fast and merry dash than a sad, slow decline. How's that the poet puts it? Did he not say: "Short and sweet as an ass's gallop"? And did not another say:

> One crowded hour of glorious life
> Is worth an age without a name.

Untapped Heat

In my youth I was acquainted with an aged bachelor who devised a unique method of heating his bed on a cold night. He did not require permanent heating, just something to start him off. He had a thing about artificial heating by such yokes as hot bottles and electric blankets.

He lived in the countryside a mere stone's throw from the main road so that he was rarely short of callers. These varied from people who had lost their way to wandering tramps and outcast itinerants. Jehovah Witnesses had still to put in an appearance in the Irish countryside at the time although there were rumours that some were about.

Anyway, when nights were frosty or when the snow blanketed the countryside or the hail tattooed window and rooftop all night long, our friend would admit an itinerant or a tramp and provide him with shelter for the night. It was the custom in the country-side in those days to allow a wandering outcast a place by the hearth until daybreak when, after a mug of tea and a boiled egg or two, he would be sent on his way and told to prey upon somebody else. It was judged to be a recipe for bad luck if he was sent hungry from the door.

Upon being informed by the aged proprietor that he would be allowed to stay the wanderer would be profuse in his thanks, calling down all of God's blessings in the most colourful fashion on his benefactor.

"Spare your thanks," my elderly bachelor friend would inform him, "and go up instead to the bedroom. Strip to the skin and warm my bed. Then come down to take your place beside the hearth."

Willingly the wanderer would disrobe in the dark bedroom and stay in the cold bed until it was warmed. Sometimes a wearier wanderer than others might fall asleep and he would have to be forcibly removed. However, most merely did what was expected of them. My ancient friend would then disrobe and dive into the warm hollow between the sheets. It was a good system. He was, I must concede, somewhat choosy about the type of person he would permit into his bed. If there was any sort of stink or whiffiness off the visitor he would not be invited to stay or if he looked too fragile and anaemic he would be considered incapable of warming any sort of bed.

The most welcome type was a large, stout, well-fleshed, middle-aged male. Firstly he would warm more of the bed than was required thereby providing the legitimate owner with considerable leeway before being obliged to vacate the warm spot. In short the replacement could stretch his legs as far as he liked without any fear of having his toes frozen. He could lie on back, belly or sides and be sure of natural warmth wherever he turned. It was a fair exchange and my friend attributed his great age to this unique heating system. There was, he would declare, nothing as beneficial as natural heat.

Women who do not share their husbands' beds take note. Send him first to warm yours before entering it.

I also remember a family who lived in our street when I was a gorsoon. One of the children was always sent upstairs at night to warm his grandmother's bed. She would be well supplied with artificial aids but she regarded the natural heat to be without peer.

For all that may be said in favour of electric blankets and hot water bottles there is nothing to equal the blissful heat of a partner's body after coming in from the cold on a winter's night.

Times Past

"We were like Adam and Eve!"

The words are Dan Heffernan's. Dan was in Listowel only last week on one of his numerous excursions from his native Islandanny and when we pressed him he rolled back the blanket of years and exposed for us once more the pure white sheets of his youth.

There were no bathing togs in Islandanny in those dear and distant days and when the youth of the neighbourhood swam and bathed in the famous Cot Hole in the crystal clear Feale river during the warm days of summer they did so in their birthday suits.

According to Dan Heffernan there was no pollution in those days and the only foreign body ever seen in the Feale River was an Italian knife thrower employed by a smalltime circus. For one reason or another he chose the bountiful Feale for his premature demise. Rumour had it that he was jilted by a beautiful slack-wire walker who transferred her affections to the aged but wealthy proprietor of the circus in question.

When Dan and his friends went frolicking in the deep of the Cot Hole their bodies were washed cleaner than whistles by the wholesome waters of this recently much-abused river.

"We were like Adam and Eve," said Dan, "and manamdeel the only togs I ever saw was a football tog."

Dan recalled how they were passed out on the road one day by one of Geary's vans while on their way to the river. At this time Geary's current tops and plain biscuits were extremely popular.

"It was the height of June," said Dan, "and if you were to go through the sky with Moll Sheahan's fine comb you wouldn't find as much as a rib of cloud."

Apparently Moll Sheahan was a woman who made the most assiduous of searches through the heads of her offspring in search of the assorted vermin which were as numerous in Dan's boyhood as were the mighty herds of bison on the great American plains when Sitting Bull was a papoose.

"Geary's van went by," said Dan, "at a fairly hot pace and when it made the turn at Sluice Quarter didn't the back door open and out fell a wooden box of currant tops. That was the greatest day of all times," said Dan, "because the following day we would be recruited for the bog to do the footing of the turf and the currant tops were a godsend."

"Sure the bog was a holiday in itself," I suggested.

"The bog was dynamite," was Dan's answer, "especially the three days' cutting. We always cut three days and at the end of that you'd have blisters on your hands like small balloons. There would be four of us to the slean, one cutting, one breenching, one pitching and one spreading."

"What about food?" I asked.

"Mixed bread and milk was all the food we got."

"And what about the four o'clock tea?" I asked.

"For the four o'clock tea," said Dan, "we got more milk."

"I suppose," said another listener, "that ye had plenty meat or maybe cheese or hardboiled eggs or the like."

Here Dan Heffernan was overcome with laughter. For a long time it looked as if he would be seized by a serious fit of convulsions but after a while the laughter subsided and Dan was his old self again.

"There was no such thing as meat," Dan explained, "or butter or cheese or hardboiled eggs or any kind of an egg. We got all the mixed bread we could eat or nearly as much and we got plenty new milk. There was no tea. Remember there was a war on and that tea was rationed."

"That time," said Dan, "you'd see fine pairs of bloomers hanging out on clothes lines to dry. They were as long and as wide as the sails of ships. I declare to God you could put a butt of spuds into the two legs. They covered everything from the breast down to the knee. I wonder what happened to them at all. They seemed only to come in three colours, white, pink and blue. The clothes lines used be festooned with them and that was the clapping and flapping when the wind would catch hold of them. No gander made the noise they made and not one left now. All you'd see now is a wisp of a thing that wouldn't make a bandage for your ludeen. By the Lord God but they were what you might call knickers long ago. Everyone wore 'em when I was a gorsoon and glad to have 'em. They were made from flour bags often and I see written on the leg of one of 'em that was worn by an old woman: 'Do Not Pat Or Shake.' The flour, you see, would rise like dust if you patted or shook the bag."

"Did people work harder in those days than they do now?" asked a schoolboy who happened to be on the premises with his mother who had come in to procure some take-away gin for a trifle.

"Work was harder," said Dan Heffernan, "but you had as many dodgers then as you have now. Often there was more work done around the fire at night than was ever done by day."

"Could you elaborate?" I asked.

"Well," said Dan, "suppose there was a field to be drained the following day they would do most of it in front of the hearth the night before. You see they would smooth the ashes all around the hearth and then the man that had the field to be drained would take hold of the tongs and he would show the way the field was to be drained. I seen them and they at it all night. Often the sweat would fall. I seen a poor woman going to town one night to bring back porter, they were working so hard around the hearth. Of course, they done damn-all the following day. It was the same with the bog. All night they'd sit in front of the hearth with the sweat falling off of 'em. There they'd be and they gone down to the seventh sod after cutting the biggest slean of turf ever seen."

"What were the hours like in the bog?"

"Well," said Dan, "it wasn't like now when you'd have to wait for a man to sign before he'd start. That time you would have to be in the bog at seven o'clock in the morning and you'd be lucky if you finished up at six in the evening. Only twice would you eat. The dinner would be around eleven o'clock, a dinner of mixed bread and new milk and then there was what they call the four o'clock tay and you got mixed bread and new milk for that as well. I never seen a sign of butter in the bog when I was a gorsoon."

"Would you sell any of the turf?"

"Oh yes, we'd all have a horse rail or two so's we'd have a few shillings for Listowel Races. Around the fall of the year we'd take a horse rail to the depot in Abbeyfeale. The depot was at the railway. Turf was bought by the weight and the money was good. It was the first real money ever made by country people."

"Who bought the turf?"

"Oh there were a lot of buyers at the Abbeyfeale depot. There was Mattie Connell and Paddy Lyons I think it was. Then there was John Curtin from the Mall."

"Where is the Mall?" asked the schoolboy.

"There was a lot of Malls," Dan answered, "but the most

famous two were the Mall in Duagh and the Mall in Knocknagoshel. There were two buyers all told from the Mall of Knocknagoshel. As well as Curtin there was Donaleen Keane."

"Would ye never wet the turf before ye took it to be weighed?"

"No," answered Dan, "for we had heavy turf but I often see a man with light turf and he'd hose it well with water for five minutes. It wouldn't be noticed if the day was wet. Often for every pound's worth of turf the buyer would be buying maybe two or three shillings worth of water."

"What else from those days worth recalling?"

"Honesty," answered Dan. "I often seen three or four eating out of the one plate and they wouldn't wrong one another a crumb."

Ecclesiastical Persifleurs

I know a man notorious for his silences in public houses and public places, renowned for his absence from the debating chamber and the meeting hall, but send him to mass of a Sunday and stand him outside the door of the church whilst the sacrifice is in progress and he will outwit and outsmart Bob Hope and Daniel O'Connell together. Away from holy ground, as it were, he is the very soul of taciturnity. Put him the simplest of questions and he'll close up like a clam. Away from his natural forum this ecclesiastical persifleur is no more than a damp squib.

But what makes him tick on church grounds? He is, of course, in possession of a captive audience. Not all churches offer outdoor forums on Sundays. There are tough priests who will not tolerate outdoor entertainment of any kind whilst the mass is under way.

I well recall my introduction to these mass-related frolics. It was a warm summer's Sunday and because our parents had attended an earlier mass there was nobody to supervise myself and a slightly older brother. With nobody to direct us we stood at the back of the church. A number of older boys and adults were already standing there and nobody objected when we decided to take up squatting rights.

After a while mass began. The brother who was never a man for confined places shuffled a good deal and wiped imaginary beads of sweat from his forehead.

"I'm sick," he whispered faintly, "you stay here till I get back."

The sermon, meanwhile, had ended and the mass proceeded slowly, the sleep-inducing, lame-legged Latin almost compelling the eyes to close.

"I am my brother's keeper," I told myself righteously as I sidled backwards out of the church. Outside it was a different world. The goings-on without bore no comparison at all to the goings-on within. All around were happily disposed men of every age, some with one knee on the ground, others seated with their backs to the wall of the church. One sly fellow surreptitiously smoked a cigarette butt whilst another ceremoniously cleaned his pipe. It was a startling change. Several conversations were in progress. There was also a good deal of mime. One young fellow with a copper-red face and a cap embroidered with fishing flies was engaged in the ancient mimicry of the fishy story.

At first I could not believe my eyes and ears. The transition from sanctity to carnival was almost too much. The biggest charade of all, to my mind, was the sight of the brother and another young buck endeavouring, vainly, to behave like all the other outdoor perverts who were shining tributes to the power of bad example.

Suddenly silence descended upon one and all. One of the priests of the parish had appeared on the scene. There was a black look on his face although he had no way of seeing me where I knelt hidden behind the ample back of a local corner boy. He had no trouble spotting the brother and another under-age transgressor. Seizing them each by an ear he ran them into the body of the church. The priest did not bother himself with the others. Old lags these, steeped in the ways of nonconformity. He shook his head in sorrow and entered the church with the terrifying disclosure that we would all rot in hell. Never again did I stand outside a church while mass was in progress.

The priest's departure was the signal for the resumption of mimes and conversations. The first presentation resulted from a heated argument concerning a goal scored in a recent football game. One of the cads involved in the dispute assumed the role of goalie and another the mantle of the hero who had scored the goal. Direction was under the auspices of a fat man who smelled of freshly consumed porter and who had set himself up as the ultimate authority on the goal in question. As the sharpshooter drew back his leg the goalie dived. The trouble was that although the sharpshooter drew back his leg he did not actually kick the ball. He sent the goalie diving in the wrong direction. After that it was child's play for the sharpshooter to finish the ball to the back of the net. It was, without doubt, superb mime. It was also the essence of scandal-giving.

Such then were the activities which took place outside the parish church of Listowel forty-five years ago. Recent attempts to revive these diabolical games have been sharply nipped in the bud although they still continue on a smaller scale, prompted and promoted by a small number of perverted wretches who don't know any better.

Resolutions

There was once a publican in Listowel whose wife made him promise that he would stop swearing as a New Year's resolution. He stopped but his business deteriorated. In addition his clientele changed. Impaired by his promise he no longer terrified unwelcome blackguards with the power and colour of his scurrilous imprecations. Thugs and villians once chastened by blistering maledictions now felt free to intimidate him and his customers. Worst of all, however, was the fact that most of his admirers, those who enjoyed and appreciated his outpourings, sought out other hostelries to be entertained.

In the end his wife relented. It was that or starve. In no time at all he was back at his old ways. His regular customers returned, the thugs and villians departed while strangers marvelled at the scope and vigour of his awful fulminations.

The moral here is that we should not assume resolutions which do more harm than good. I remember I myself once went off drink for the New Year. It was a difficult undertaking but I persevered despite sleepless nights and an indescribable longing for the few pints of beer which had been my nightcap for so long. In the end a delegation, consisting of my entire family, approached me and begged me to terminate my resolution on the grounds that I was making life unbearable for each and every one of them. Hard, apparently, as my decision had been for me it had been infinitely worse for them.

Then there was the relation of mine, a chap of seventy from the Stacks Mountains, who rose out of whiskey as the saying goes and took to drinking minerals. He lost every rib of hair on his head. His false teeth became too large for his gums and he lost his appetite for food. At the instigation of his family he fell back on the whiskey. His teeth fitted perfectly. He regained his appetite but not a solitary rib of hair returned to take the bare look from his head.

New Year's resolutions as we have shown through the foregoing illustrations, while always commendable, should never be undertaken lightly.

Not long after I was introduced to my first pint of stout I went off the drink for the New Year. At the time I could not have been more than eighteen. Most of my friends went off the drink as well and we successfully maintained our resolutions across the winter until Saint Patrick's Day matured into night and we resumed our old habits, i.e., the consumption of two or three pints of stout on Holy nights and Sunday nights to put us in form for the dance.

The more vocal apostles of temperance might insist that he was a very demoralised and unstable character indeed who required intoxicating liquor before a dance but be that as it may, we nevertheless found our weekly visits to the pub both uplifting and exciting and the liquor itself an ideal stimulant for participation in the Terpsichorean art. In fact there were some of my companions who could not face up to a dancing partner without the aid of at least two pints of stout. Upholders of temperance might maintain that there was a serious psychological deficiency here somewhere but I would suggest that a short visit to a public house is a lot less expensive than a visit to a psychologist and in many cases more beneficial so where does that leave us?

When we went off the drink in that distant time we were following a pattern which existed for generations. There are and were many who went off the booze for the month of November in deference to departed kinfolk loosely described in clerical terms as the holy souls. Others abstained for the Lenten period to emphasise their affinity with the Christian spirit of self denial. Of course there are degrees of abstinence just as there are degrees of everything else and I well remember two chronic topers who regularly went off the strong stuff on New Year's Day only to go on something else. This, fair play to them, was a common enough practice of the period.

One would have expected them to opt for minerals such as orange or lemonade or ginger ale but this was far from the case. One might even have expected them to steer clear of public houses and thus steer clear of temptation but this was also far from the case.

In normal times their round would consist of two small whiskies and two pints of stout, the whiskey to pave the way for the stout as it were and the stout to counteract the evil effects of the whiskey by diluting it. There was a name at the time for this combination of whiskey and stout. It was called a boilermaker. The whiskey was swallowed first, neat and whole, and was followed immediately by a substantial gulp of the stout. It was a highly stimulating beverage but men who worked hard would argue that they needed such potent draughts to restore energies lost during the round of a demanding day.

One thing must be said in defence of this pair before we go any further. They had neither wives nor children. One had lost his spouse through illness whilst the other had never made the slightest attempt to acquire one. They had no other dependants that I can recall.

Anyway New Year's Day came around and our pair of abstainers failed to show up at their local pub. They were sorely missed because at that time employment was even scarcer than it is now and most of the young men were far away in England or America so that publicans were at their wits' ends to make a go of things.

Now there was at the farthest end of town a small, uninhabited pub. When I say uninhabited I mean that it was rarely peopled by customers and it was here that our two friends decided to spend their period of so-called abstention. This period never lasted longer than ten or twelve days. One night out of curiosity a few of us decided to look in on them with a view to finding out how they were faring. We were somewhat surprised to see glasses of intoxicating liquor on the counter in front of them. There was neither whiskey nor stout, their accustomed drenches, but there were worthy substitutes.

Each had before him what looked suspiciously like a glass of port and a pint of cider. As we entered they were engaged in earnest conversation with a small, grey-haired lady who was seated behind the counter. She was darning a black sock but this in no way hampered her participation in the conversation. If memory serves me correctly the subject under discussion was the vile weather which obtained at the time. The conversation grew even more earnest when our friends perceived who had entered.

Eventually we availed of an opening so we put it to the pair of port and cider drinkers that they had broken their New Year's resolutions. They merely scoffed at this, pointing out that wine was only a woman's drink and that cider was only a gorsoon's drink. Therefore, neither collectively nor individually did they come under the heading of hard drink.

So saying they lifted their glasses of port and disposed of them at one swallow after first sloshing the wine around in their mouths with great satisfaction. They then forced it in and out between their teeth before allowing it backwards and downwards to its true destination. They then turned their attention to the cider which they swallowed with great gusto until their glasses were half empty.

"You'd miss the oul' drop of the hot stuff," said one to the other.

"You would indeed," said he, "to say nothing about the sup of porter."

In their own eyes their New Year's resolutions were still intact and would be intact until they returned to their native drinking haunts, there to partake of whiskey and stout for the remainder of the year.

Booze Transporters

It was the evening of August the fifteenth, nineteen forty-nine, in the lovely seaside resort of Ballybunion. Dusk was about to be invoiced from the west by a quickly dropping sun. The main street swarmed with humanity but only one figure caught the eye. She was a shawled tinker woman, lithe enough of frame but with a face which carried the scrawls of numerous beatings. Inside the shawl she carried what seemed to be an infant.

Although patently drunk so great was her concern for her tender charge that all her staggers righted themselves before she could come a cropper. I watched her with admiration as she staggered from one end of the street to the other without once allowing her babe to be bruised. The creature was a known drunkard, a martyr to alcoholic drinks of all sorts.

As I watched her retreating from view I was joined by another member of the travelling community.

"Fair play to her," I said, "she's looking after the child well."

"Child!" he echoed scornfully. "She'd never pay that much attention to a child. That's a gallon of porter."

I have always been intrigued by the transport of booze from pub to party or from pub to home. Men and women sated with alcohol, who might otherwise fall to the ground, manage somehow to remain upright until their destinations have been reached because of the precious nature of the commodity they transport. If they were not the bearers of booze they would surely suffer serious injury: but so great is their devotion to the containers they carry that they will contort and reanimate themselves beyond their known physical limitations rather then jeopardise their cargoes.

There was a short-sighted cousin of my own, an undistinguished fellow if ever there was one in all respects except in his singular devotion to all makes of alcohol. Drunk though he might be he could always be relied upon to transport a dozen of stout and a few noggins of the hot stuff to any given destination regardless of the distance and regardless of his condition. There may have been soberer persons present to whom the precious consignment might have been entrusted but they were not nearly as reliable as my drunken relation.

One night the inevitable happened. A hard frost had earlier imposed itself on a wet roadway and it was while crossing same that he skidded and fell. It was the only fall in a lifetime conveying intoxicating liquor from one place to another. When he fell he fell heavily, banging his head off the roadway. He lay stunned for a while and then he extended a shaky hand to examine the terrain around him. He was horrified when his fingers discovered rivulets of liquid on the frozen surface close by.

"Tell me it's only blood," he called out to a concerned companion who had come to his aid. In what other pursuit would you find such devotion and loyalty? I submit that for action above and beyond the call of duty your genuine drunkard is without peer when it comes to looking after his hooch.

I remember another relative who also suffered from the alcoholic affliction. To him icy roads never presented a hazard because while transporting booze he utilised a shuffle which he had painstakingly developed over the years. It was a shuffle especially calculated to adapt to any terrain. He might be the last to arrive at the party but when he did arrive his cargo was intact. I once saw him severely tested.

He was a man with poor sight and as a result was obliged to wear spectacles with strong lenses. One night while transporting a larger than usual consignment of liquor the spectacles fell down over his nose so that his vision was seriously impaired.

Let me explain here that he had not loaded the booze upon himself. It had been loaded upon him by another and could only be unloaded by another. He could not therefore lay it upon the ground so that he could right his glasses. If he did he would be forced to leave some of his cargo behind. For him this would have been a serious dereliction, the ultimate in betrayal.

What he did was to stand still, holding on firmly to all his bottles until some other human should pass. He was obliged to wait for the best part of an hour but this he did with commendable fortitude. When another toper happened to pass the way he hailed him and asked him to right his spectacles. This the other drunkard managed to do with considerable difficulty. Drunk as he was he fully understood my relative's dilemma. It would have been unthinkable to either to abandon even a solitary drop of the cargo.

The moral is that if these conveyors of alcohol had opted for other less punishing pursuits they would surely have ended up captains of industry or masters of art. They, however, were content with what they were and never asked for recognition.

Of Cats and Cuckoos

I would respectfully suggest to all those who write to me from time to time concerning the manufacture of humorous essays to look to the gentle cuckoo for inspiration. The cuckoo has written only one essay and that unique effort has to do with the advent of summer. It is the shortest essay ever written and this is why he is entitled to repeat it hour after hour until such time as he feels disposed towards returning to his native Morocco.

Let us suppose that you have undertaken to compose an essay about the advent of summer. I do not say that you should set out to accomplish it in two words the same as the cuckoo. First you would be well advised to read what other essayists had to say and if you cannot create an original piece yourself there is no harm in assimilating the findings of those you have read and in trying to distil same into a brief and expressive appreciation of the summer scene.

The achievement of a man who overwrites an essay is just about as valueless as that of a losing horse who reserves his best gallop for when he passes the winning post. My advice is to mark well the cuckoo's brevity, his fluency and his total commitment to economy. Never repeat yourself, however.

You may be sure that the cuckoo did not learn to say "cuckoo" overnight. Neither does a man learn to write essays in an afternoon although there was a great essay written on the spur of the moment, an essay so memorable that it deserves to be set aside as a blueprint. While it could not truthfully be said that it matches the cuckoo's conciseness it nevertheless has a magic all of its own.

As far as I recall I came across the collation whilst reading a paperback by the inimitable Paddy Crosbie of *School Around the Corner* fame. Readers may not agree that it is the definitive work I make it out to be, the essay that is, but I genuinely feel that the comparison should be recorded. To the best of my recollection Paddy Crosbie was reminiscing at the time about essays he had come across in his time as a schoolmaster. He recalled one class of eleven-year-old girls in particular. He explained to the class, beforehand, the vital elements of a good composition which, I daresay, is a junior essay. He advised them to be brief, to the point and above all to stick to the subject. We all know how girls of that age can ramble on and on and on.

The subject of the composition on this occasion was the household cat or to be more familiar and less didactic he instructed them to write under the title: "Our Cat". Many of the compositions were rambling and wordy and strayed away from the subject altogether whilst others were unimaginative although few were dull. Then unexpectedly a gem appeared near the bottom of the dwindling heap of copybooks. There is always one.

The eleven-year-old Dublin girl who wrote it must have been genuinely inspired. Certainly she had the makings of a classical essayist. It was the shortest essay by far of the whole caboodle and this is all it said:

"Our Cat. We had a cat but we thrun him out."

It was all there in that one sentence. It told the reader everything he wanted to know about the cat in question. I have known cats like that cat but not completely like him. He was their cat all right and he was different.

Another sentence would be merely to gild the lily. I wish I had written an essay like it in my time. I read that essay again and again. It was too mature to be labelled a mere composition. That eleven-year-old girl and the cuckoo are the only creatures I have known to have created natural masterpieces out of tricky subjects. Ponder it well. Remember the words and you'll see that cat and that family.

"We had a cat but we thrun him out."

Funeral Capers

I would now like to devote a few lines to the subject of funerals, mourners and sympathisers. Indeed I might not be doing so at all were it not for the fact that I was at a funeral recently where the sympathisers made every effort to knock one another down. I never saw such heedless and wanton horseplay. Then I heard a voice whisper in my ear: "You'd badly want to write something about this." I looked around and beheld an old schoolmate of mine who, like myself, was caught up in the mad scramble.

"'Tis like a New Year sale," said a small female who was in constant danger of being annihilated. Indeed it was. The behaviour of at least half of those present was bordering on hooliganism. But let me recall a particular funeral before proceeding with the subject of funeral behaviour.

It's more than a few years ago now. It was one o'clock of a Sunday afternoon. Kerry were playing Cork in Cork for the Munster football title and the man who had promised me a lift to the game had just rung up to say that his wife was having premature labour pains and that a blessed event was likely to take place at any minute. So there I was, stranded, sitting dolefully on my own window-sill with little likelihood of a lift at that late stage. I had more or less resigned myself to an afternoon with the radio when down the street in his station wagon came my friend and neighbour Jerome Murphy. When he saw me he pulled up.

"I thought you'd be at the match," he said.

"I would too," I responded, "but Mickeen's wife's time has come and he cannot go but maybe you might be going yourself?"

"I'm not going," he informed me, "but where I am going is to a funeral in Duagh." Having said this he sat in the car for a moment eyeing me speculatively.

"Sit in," he said finally. "All I have to do is drop into the chapel to sympathise. We'll just make the game if we move lively."

Thus it was that I found myself standing at the entrance to Duagh church awaiting the exit of Jerome who had gone in a few moments previously to extend his condolences to the next of kin. People were still arriving for the funeral and one of these, a crafty-looking gent with a zipped-up gansey and peaked cap, hardly a July garb, approached me and seized my right hand firmly in his. Others who followed in his wake did exactly the same thing. They seized my hand, each and every one of them and they shook it for all they were worth muttering expressions of sympathy such as "sorry for your trouble," "he made a good battle" and "he's in Heaven now". There was no use in protesting.

These people, the majority of whom did not know me any more than the sky over me, were determined to have the condolences done with. A few, instead of continuing on into the church, simply turned on their heels after shaking my hand and skedaddled in the belief that they had done their duty by the deceased. They too were on their way to Cork. I quickly returned to the car lest the hand be shaken off me. Make no mistake about it, a would-be sympathiser, especially if he or she is in a hurry, will sympathise with anybody who happens to be contiguous to the church, the coffin or the grave.

I once had a relation who used to say, "I don't know what carries some people to funerals. They cannot be seen and, therefore, they make trips in vain. As for me now, you will always note me thirty yards ahead of the hearse where every man, woman and child, barring the dead man alone, can see me as plain as the day. My policy is if you're not going to be seen you might as well stay at home."

I once saw a man knocked to the ground outside Listowel's parish church of a winter's night about ten years ago. He was old and he was feeble and his only crime was that he resembled the chief mourners who had earlier pulled a fast one on the crowd by hightailing it into the church before they could be sympathised with.

Mistakenly some short-sighted sympathiser shook the hand of the elderly man already mentioned. He might not be too closely related to the deceased but he would do well enough and he would be sure to inform the proper authorities later on regarding the identities of those who had shaken hands with him. After that initial handshake the poor creature was inundated. There was nobody else available and, as the saying goes, any old port will do in a storm. At the heel of the hunt the poor fellow was knocked down. His age, his fragility and the few half whiskies he had consumed were contributory factors to his downfall but the real criminals were the over-enthusiastic mourners who simply wanted the unpleasant ordeal of sympathising over and done with.

It was Tacitus the Roman historian writing two thousand years ago who said, among other things, that the Celts were great people for attending funerals. We haven't changed much in the intervening years and more power to us. Of course it is always heartening for those left behind to see the deceased sent off in style. Often enough in our long and often lonely history there were many who had only a foursome to bear them to the grave and there were some who had less.

The thing I most object to is when large crowds suddenly converge upon a handful of weak or elderly mourners with a view to shaking the hands off them. They remind me of nothing but a litter of excited greyhounds the minute the luckless hare is sighted. The mourners, like the hare, are regarded as fair game and are often chased with the same zeal and velocity. At the same time sympathy has to be expressed. What then is a sympathiser to do? First of all he must take his time and advance upon the next of kin in a reserved and stately manner. He must remember that he is not in a competition and very often, although I am reluctant to point it out, women are the worst culprits. They will pinch and push and shove, not to mind queue-jumping, in order to edge an inch or two nearer to the corpse. I myself have often been ruthlessly pushed aside by small, determined, robust women who would be a credit to a rugby pack.

What's really wanted, of course, is a referee who would blow his whistle loudly the moment he spots unfair shoving or pushing or indeed tripping and elbowing. Then with hand outstretched he would seize the culprit, male or female, and make them stand aside until the cortege moves away.

Then comes a lull in the sympathising while the Rosary is being recited. Intending handshakers scrape and stamp their feet impatiently, unable to keep still. To them the five decades seem as long as eternity. They look anxiously about them fearful lest the chance to seize a hand might slip. When the Rosary comes to an end there is a stampede. There is total disregard for the welfare of the weaker people present. Nothing matters but the corralling of the defenceless next of kin in the shortest time possible by any means possible.

Although often quite close to the next of kin myself I have frequently moved to one side lest I be trampled or maimed. At the same time it must be conceded that if a man comes a long way to a funeral the fact must somehow be conveyed to the chief mourners and what better way than by approaching them and confronting them with one's presence. Unfortunately, because of the battering they have received, the mourners are very often dazed and bewildered and have the greatest difficulty in identifying unfamiliar faces.

Corner Boys 2

People often question my fascination with corners and corner boys. Some ask if I ever write about anything else while more insist that I am biased against corner boys.

"I honestly believe," a woman once said to me as we conversed in the vicinity of the Castle Green in Ballybunion, "you'd love to be a corner boy yourself but you don't have the courage."

This is not strictly true since I am, like most townspeople, a part-time corner boy. Often when I have nothing better to do I'll stand at a corner or if I want to know the result of a local football match I'll ask one of the resident corner boys.

No, my fascination with corner boys springs from one simple fact and it is that there is a corner across the road from me. If a man lives at the foot of a mountain he is sure to be influenced by the mountain or if a man lives by the side of a lake that lake is sure to occupy his thoughts a good deal of the time. Thus it is with me and with corners. I simply cannot ignore my neighbourhood corner.

Whenever I see a man standing at a corner I try to fathom his reasons for being there. In most cases a man standing at a corner is simply a corner boy. He stands there for the greater part of the day every day of the week. There are others, however, who do no more than meet at corners. To these, corners are convenient landmarks. These interlopers are easily identified. They are never done with examining their timepieces. They fret, fume and stamp fruitlessly on the pavements when the expected party fails to appear. They will never be true corner boys. They lack the patience and the fortitude.

It is seldom one sees a female supporting a corner. In fact there is no such thing as a corner girl. Sometimes, of course, I notice a country woman standing patiently at a corner with bags of groceries waiting for somebody to show up, a husband or a son or a neighbour. After a while it is easy to see that she is stranded. Most likely she had arranged with her husband to meet at a certain corner after she had bought the week's groceries but because of those faulty communications which so often exist between the most companionable of husbands and wives she has chosen the wrong corner. It happens every day of the week. It might not be too bad if it happened in a small town or village where there are few corners or only one corner. In a large town there are many corners and the woman with the groceries may have to hang on for hours on end while her husband eliminates corner after corner until, eventually, he finds the right one. It is not always a happy reunion. Tempers, for the most part his, are generally frayed by the time contact is made.

Last week I witnessed a strange phenomenon at the corner which stands directly across the street from my study. There is no day that something does not happen at this corner. It is the town's busiest corner for one thing and it has other features which attract all kinds of passers-by. It is bright and bustling and roomy, three primary essentials for any corner.

Now to our phenomenon. At about eleven thirty in the morning a man arrived at the corner. He was tall and thin. He was long-jawed and unwashed. He wore a peaked cap, spectacles and a long, well-worn overcoat. He wore wellingtons with their tops turned down. He was, all in all, a pretty unprepossessing sight. For a while I thought he was some unfortunate rustic who had lost his way. However, when he failed to ask the resident corner boy for directions I knew that I had put the wrong tag on him.

Meanwhile the phone rang and I answered it. When I returned my man was still there. By this time he looked more relaxed. He had thrust his hands into the pockets of his overcoat and was leaning contentedly against the corner. The resident corner boy eyed him dispassionately and moved to the other side of the corner where he made a careful examination of the terrain before finally choosing a part of the corner against which he might lean without obstructing the general public.

I knew the newcomer by sight and I had a good idea of where he hailed from. He was, as far as I knew, of the single persuasion and resided in a run-down cottage about three miles from the town and a lengthy jaunt in from the main road. I also knew from neighbouring farmers that he was a man who had sworn off all kinds of work several years before on the grounds that he was persecuted by an itincrant pain in the back. I estimated that he was just beginning to find the countryside too desolate and that he had decided to have a shot at life in town.

The next time I looked he was in the act of offering a conciliatory cigarette to the resident corner boy. The latter accepted it with alacrity and soon the pair were conversing amicably.

Corner lore is a fascinating study with its own rules and regulations. It is a known fact that if a resident corner boy takes a shine to an intruder he may very well adopt him and invite him to share his corner. A good corner can cater for several boys. Soon other corner boys began to arrive. Finally there were five altogether and they were in a playful mood.

For the most part corner boys do nothing but lean against corners but on this occasion they were putting on a show. When it became obvious that the intruder was not willing to hand out any more cigarettes they proceeded to give him the cold shoulder by not including him in their games which consisted chiefly of playful sparring, executing short dances and buckleaps, whispering to each other about the intruder and laughing loudly at each other's disclosures. When they had laughed their fills they scratched themselves gleefully under the arms and tweaked their noses as well as slapping their thighs with their hands.

It was all too much for the intruder who had never been initiated into the rites of the corner boy system. He slunk away disheartened and demoralised. He would never be a corner boy. He had been rebuffed. Only one course was open to him: find a corner of his own. Alas the waiting list is so long that an aspirant might be dead before a vacancy occurred.

What harm but he had the posture and composure of a true corner boy but as with entry to many careers, it is not what you know but who you know. Maybe if he had been properly introduced by an experienced corner boy who would have paved the way for him beforehand the story might have been different.

What he had undergone during his visit to the corner was a sort of initiation ceremony. If he had endured the humiliation to which he had been subjected he might have gone on in time to be a distinguished corner boy.

So we end this particular chapter on corner boys and corners. It was a story of rejection and failure but if it did nothing more than alert aspiring corner boys to the pitfalls of the profession it has served a useful purpose.

Food for Thought

When I was a gorsoon an accomplished farmer's boy had to be able to foot and clamp turf. In those days turf sheds were almost unknown and the reek had to be well constructed as well as closely clamped.

No one stole from a well-clamped reek. It was from the carelessly-clamped, crumbling reeks that the turf-stealer filled his bag or rail. Even a single sod would be missed from a well clamped reek whereas a collapsed reek was considered fair game for turf thieves.

A farmer's boy had also to be able to castrate calves and bonhams. He had to be able to dose cattle, dehorn bullocks, paint dwelling-houses and outhouses and be something of an interior decorator to boot. Possessed though he might be of all these gifts he could still find himself without a job if he was not also as strong as the proverbial horse.

If he wasn't strong his mother would be obliged to take him to town to find a job for him as a counter-hand or clerk. If she was very lucky she might succeed in getting him a job in an office but you needed contacts for this. Contacts, however, cut no ice with your North Kerry farmer. Practical realist that he was your North Kerry farmer had his own method for judging the suitability of a candidate for a postion on his farm.

On rare occasions when he was asked by a politician to give a job to a voter he would promise to see what could be done but laugh later on to himself at the absurdity of such a thing. It was one thing to squander the state's monies on poorly qualified appointees but there was no way a farmer could afford to indulge in such lunacies.

The best credentials a farmer's boy could possibly possess were superhuman strength allied to the most meagre of appetites plus a superabundance of farming skills without too high a degree of intelligence. The last thing a farmer required was an enlightened or educated assistant. These tended to agitate rather than work and, strangely enough, a well-educated farmer's boy always managed to eat more than a less enlightened farmer's boy even though the latter might have worked twice as hard.

It would appear, therefore, that all forms of thinking, pondering, agitating, arguing and disputing can be more demanding than physical labour and it is a widely known truth that those who do no work at all can more than hold their own at the table with those who work like slaves. There is an interesting thesis here for advanced students of human psychology and what really suprises me is that the medical profession has provided no explanation so far.

I have seen positive proof of this when I used to visit the local boglands for the purpose of cutting my year's supply of peat. I have seen men work like Trojans from morning till night and yet eat not a scrap more than dodgers who feigned exhaustion and illness all day. In fact the slackers would sometimes complain that there was not enough food to go around and would go so far as to suggest that committed workers should surrender some of their vittles to the work-shy convalescents.

As I say it's a most mystifying business entirely. It has baffled me for years and has genuinely puzzled many householders who provide daily rations for all sorts of bogland workers.

For instance, there is a lady of my acquaintance who has two sons, both sound in wind and limb and lacking nothing in intelligence. The older is employed and works a long, hard day for his wages. The other does no work at all. Yet when the pair take to the table the non-worker easily outclasses the hard-working brother. In fact, when the working brother pushes away his plate the non-worker consumes anything the worker might have overlooked. The worker is also less choosy about his food whereas the non-worker is faddy and fussy and forever complaining about the quantity and the quality of what's put in front of him.

The whole business is most puzzling surely and needs the sort of in-depth investigation which only professional teams of examiners can provide. It has proved to be far too much for me and for those who continually provide food for slackers.

In-Laws

I remember to have dealt somewhere once with an outbreak of in-law trouble and a few hours later I was taken to task by a female acquaintance for making light of a very serious business. Apparently she conducts a non-stop war with most of her in-laws and maintains an uneasy truce with the remainder.

"You think it's funny," she said, "but I see nothing funny in in-laws." She listed crime after crime, injustice after injustice perpetrated against her over the years by in-laws as heartless as a graveyard full of skeletons.

The difference between the two of us is that I refuse to take my in-laws seriously whenever there is an in-law outbreak. The reason I refuse to be drawn is that in-law rifts often last a lifetime and I am happy to be able to say that I am on friendly terms with brothers-in-law and sisters-in-law who have severed diplomatic relations indefinitely with other in-laws.

I will make one concession to the lady who took me to task and that is that outsiders should be prepared in some way before they visit houses where in-law strife is rife. They might be notified by letter or by phone so that the stress and tensions which accompany in-law instability might not come as too much of a shock.

The most sensitive areas of in-law hysteria are, of course, wakes and weddings and while an outward semblance of calm might be apparent there is nevertheless under the surface a seething and highly inflammable danger area from which trouble could erupt without warning.

Having admitted that I do not take in-law warring seriously I am prepared to concede that it can be the bane of other people's lives and I might be prepared to erect a danger sign where there is a likelihood of a serious outbreak, that is to say an outbreak which might upset the tranquility and enjoyment of innocent bystanders. All the same, many wise people firmly hold that all bystanders are fair game for the good reason that a person who stands when he might vamoose is more curious than innocent.

Alas I digress a little and for this I apologise. Let us proceed from now on without further interference of an irrelevant nature. I would, as I said, be prepared to see a danger sign erected where there is a long and serious history of in-law incontinence. A simple sign might be the most effective like: "In-Law Trouble Here." Or more simple still what about: "Caution, Dangerous In-Laws Ahead".

Let me say before I proceed further that only in-laws can solve in-law trouble and secondly that it cannot be solved permanently. Any outside person who attempts to make the peace has no chance of success; not even gentlemen of the cloth. The advice I would give to those who mean well is the same that I myself was given by my grand-uncle many years ago during a wake.

Two sets of sisters-in-law were at it hammer and tongs. I was about to ask them to cool it but he wisely restrained me by the simple expedient of thrusting a glass of whiskey into my upraised hand.

"Son," said he, "let 'em at it." How right that old man was. In time the outbreak subsided and the wake continued in peace and harmony. If I had not let them at it who knows what would have happened.

I would venture to say at this juncture that the great poet, Alexander Pope had in-law outbreaks in mind when he penned the immortal line: "For fools rush in where angels fear to tread!"

I don't care how erudite the would-be intermediary is or how vast his experience of the human condition. He is a fool if he thinks he can put down an in-law uprising.

How's that Alexander Pope put it again?

The blissful blockhead ignorantly read
With loads of learned lumber in his head.

In-law in-fighting, it should be said, is almost always confined to sisters-in-law and not to daughters-in-law and mothers-in-law as we have been led to believe. There is a simple solution when trouble arises between the latter. Separate them and the trouble comes instantly to an end whereas with sisters-in-law, although they may live apart, there is non-stop recrimination of an indes-tructible character. No sooner is one wound healed than another is opened. It is the law of the in-law. There has to be non-stop instability. Maybe the great God willed it so to spare us from some other malignant form of insanity.

I remember as a small boy I was once at a wedding where the guests were mostly in-laws and where, surprisingly enough, there was no disturbance till very late in the evening. Unwittingly it was myself who contributed most to the outbreak. A middle-aged, female relative called me to one side while the festivities were at their height and asked me a number of questions relating to my family. These were of a harmless nature and she terminated the interview by handing me a half crown, a princely sum in those distant days. I am happy to say that we parted most amicably.

Shortly afterwards one of her numerous sisters-in-law, who happened to be present on the occasion, drew me to one side also. She was a blocky, black-haired bustling rampager of a woman but small and blocky as she was, she was not as small and blocky as the woman who presented me with the half crown.

When the rampager had me safely cornered she spoke to me as follows: "What," said she, "did that Dexter say about me?"

Older readers will remember the tiny cows of the Dexter breed which were plentiful in rural Ireland until recently. It was common to call small women Dexters although not always derogatorily.

"I don't remember her saying anything about you," I answered truthfully. "Honestly," I told her, "I don't remember."

"Did she say anything bad?" she asked.

"No, no," I replied hastily.

"She said nothing good I'll warrant."

"She said nothing good," I agreed and before I could emphasise that the accused said nothing bad either she was on her way to confront the poor woman who gave me the half crown. After several minutes of fiery exchanges the pair bore down upon me to settle the question one way or the other. I had no choice but to beat a hasty retreat.

My advice to those embroiled in in-law strife is to stay with it if they find it too demanding to do otherwise. Stay with it and enjoy it. Do not let it consume you, however, but keep the tormenting faces of those who irritate you most in front of you when other baser thoughts infringe upon your natural dignity. If in-laws cannot be enjoyed through respect and affection let them be enjoyed for their deficiencies.

You must not, however, expect unconnected or unrelated parties to be sympathetic or to be involved in any way. Your in-laws, in short, are not my in-laws. They are yours and yours alone. You took them on the day you or yours married into them. I have enough of my own and have no need of yours much as I would like to assist those who are over-strained by theirs.

In-law baiting, while unnerving and distressing for the subject, is of immense therapeutic value to those who might otherwise display unprovoked hostility to neighbours' children, neighbours' cats, neighbours' noises, neighbours' tantrums, neighbours' hedges and in rural areas to neighbours fowl, asses, ponies, cows, calves and other livestock.

The Bible clearly states that we must love our neighbours but there is nothing in the Bible about loving our in-laws.

We have often heard the question, "What are friends for?" The answer, of course, is to help one another. One might also ask what are in-laws for? I would suggest they are there to keep us on our toes, to remind us of our imperfections and to bring us rudely down to earth whenever we tend to fly too high.

So long as we do unto in-laws as they do unto us all will be well. It is when we lie down and surrender that the real trouble begins. Life needs its fair share of turbulence and turmoil to make it wholesome so we must conclude that a life without in-law interference is no more than a dog's life.

What Colour Are Your Wife's Eyes?

Each night they'd fight
As to which of them was right
About the colour of her eyes and hair.

(Percy French)

Those were the days. The other night I heard an old man asking a young man if he knew the colour of his wife's eyes.

"How do I know," said the scoundrel, "what colour of eyes she have?"

Two other young men came quickly to the fellow's aid by intimating that they did not know the colour of their wives' eyes either.

"I'm not exactly certain," said another, "but I think they're blue."

"Yes," said the oldster, "but what kind of blue?"

"Ordinary blue," said the young man.

"Ordinary blue!" the oldster echoed in disbelief. "Are they blue like duckeggs," he asked, "or are they Caribbean blue?"

Then he cocked his head to one side thoughtfully. "Or maybe," said he, "they might be navy blue or robin's egg blue or would they, by any chance, be puce or purple and you're ashamed to say it or maybe 'tis how they're lavender blue or even plum blue?"

The question left the young man dumbfounded and regretting he had not done his homework regarding his wife's orbs.

As I sat I recalled that my own wife's eyes are celestial blue with hints and tints of sapphire and aquamarine. Of course, I wrote a poem once to my wife's eyes in our distant days of courtship. That's the one great advantage in being a bit of a poet. You'll always notice the colour of a woman's eyes. The poet has mighty powers of observation.

There were, therefore, in our company two young men who did not know the colours of their wives' eyes. The oldster addressed himself to a middle-aged man wearing a peaked cap and welling-ton boots. He had just entered the premises and was waiting delivery of one pint of stout.

"Tell us Patcheen," asked the oldster, "what are the colour of the missus's eyes?"

"I'll be danged if I can remember," Patcheen answered, taking off his cap and scratching his head. "If it was the colour of her hair now I'd have no bother telling you because the colour is ordinary grey although I must say it wasn't always grey."

Then another man entered, a strong farmer, a close-mouthed fellow renowned for his addiction to hard work and little play. He ordered whiskey and water and while he waited impatiently for the tincture to be dispensed he was addressed by the oldest member.

"Well Miko," said he, "and what colour is your wife's eyes?"

Miko, dour as a rule, grinned hugely and when the grin sub-sided it was replaced by a generous, although uncharacteristic, smile. One could see that the old man had touched on a subject near to Miko's heart.

"My wife's eyes," said he, "are the very same in colour as forget-me-nots."

After this the oldster questioned two others but was rebuffed by both. One even resorted to a four letter word while the other simply looked the other way as though the spot where he looked held some vista of rare beauty.

It would seem from the questions posed by the old man and the answers he received that a very large percentage of husbands are not aware of the coloration of their wives' peepers and in this respect we should be thoroughly ashamed of ourselves. It also may well be true of the world at large and, if it is, it is surely a cause for concern. We should all ask ourselves, without further delay, what colour our wives' eyes are and if we are not able to answer we should do something about it.

In fact, we should hasten homewards straightaway and seize our partners firmly by the shoulders or preferably by the waists and then proceed to take a long, intense look at their optics. In reassuring ourselves of their depth and colour our spouses will also be reassured of renewed interest and of love for those female orbs, blue, green or brown, which have transmitted so many tender messages of love and forgiveness over the years.

The Power of Prayer

For what are men better than sheep or goats,
That nourish a blind life within the brain,
If knowing God, they lift not hands of prayer,
Both for themselves and those who call them friends?
For so the whole round earth is every way
Bound by gold chains about the feet of God.

(Tennyson)

Man has always underrated the power of prayer. Man has often ignored prayer and he has often scoffed at prayer because as much as man has achieved 'and as much as man understands he will never fully comprehend the power of prayer. A mother, on the other hand, is possessed of absolute faith in the power of prayer and she will resort to it with hope and confidence for the advancement and preservation of her flock and, indeed, for any other soul who may be in trouble. While she has the Rosary beads in her hands there is, in short, no holding her and you may be sure that no one will be short of a prayer whilst she is in the throes of entreaty.

Ye all know me! I was never a man to make a statement without buttressing and shaping that same pronouncement with illustration. So let me set the scene.

A large, gross, unprepossessing man of middle years lurched into my licensed premises a few weeks back and staggered blindly from one end of the bar to the other before eventually collapsing in a sprawling heap in the most comfortable corner available.

By any reckoning this unpremeditated piece of navigation was a most extraordinary feat. Consider first the fact that he was unbelievably drunk. Secondly take into account that his eyes were closed. Thirdly it should be remembered that he had never been on the premises before. Fourthly, and finally, as though it were the prelude to the long succession of snores which followed he unexpectedly broke wind with a ferocity and fervour which startled and unnerved all the other customers in the place.

Here under my very eyes was happening the one thing I loathed and despised most of all, i.e., a visit from a lout who had done his drinking in other hostelries and then, when he could drink no more, had the gall to select mine for a sleep. Oh the rank injustice of it! I raged to the ultimate. I dashed from behind the counter lest the ruffian lapse irretrievably into a drunken coma.

"Now, now," I declared with all the authority I could muster, "you'll not make a pigsty out of these here premises."

Having said this I endeavoured to lift him to his feet with a view to dispatching him as far as possible from where he now reposed. My best efforts were in vain. It was as though he were anchored to the spot where he sat. A thorough disgust seized hold of me and with it a rage that made my blood boil. Here was this inebriated interloper, this befuddled boozer, this tormenting toper occupying a choice area of my premises without consuming as much as a solitary bottle of stout under my roof.

"Up!" I shouted and I redoubled my efforts. "Up you crapulous cad before I boot you to Kingdom Come!"

Alas and alack I might as well have tried to move the Black Rocks in Ballybunion to the distant sands of Beale. I decided upon a different tack. I braced myself, spread my legs apart and thrust them where the floor and the wall join together the better to find purchase. Then I took his hands in mine and heaved with all my might, straining every muscle and exerting every ounce. Something would have to give sooner or later, I told myself, and it wasn't going to be me. There was, unfortunately, no response from the blubbery mass at the other end, nothing save the contented snores and rumbles of a man lost in the oblivion of drunken slumber.

At length I was obliged to leave go. I was determined, however, not to surrender. Most of the energy had been drained from me by now and I needed to have my batteries recharged. I also pondered my next move. Whilst all this had been happening the other patrons had been interested spectators. They seemed to be highly amused by the goings-on. Their sympathies, of course, lay with the interloper. You'd swear he was the underdog and I the bully. Of course that's the general public for you. Unless their own position is threatened they'll never take the side of the legitimate authority.

I tried to see the humorous side of it. I recalled the time Groucho Marx was playing the part of a doctor in one of his earlier films. His patient lay lifeless on the couch when Groucho entered wearing a white coat and harnessed with an outsize stethoscope. He lifted the patient's hand carelessly so that the pulse could be recorded. Groucho stood for a long time, the patient's wrist in his hand. Every so often he would look at his watch.

"Well doctor?" asked a pretty nurse who stood in attendance.

"Either this man is dead," Groucho answered, "or my watch is stopped."

I stood silently surveying my own patient. I sought in vain for a method of awakening and ejecting him. During the time he had been seated a number of potential customers had come and gone, rejecting the premises out of hand because of the presence of our obese friend. Something had to be done and done soon if trade was to be maintained and morale redeemed.

He broke wind secondly much to the amusement of all present. Then an elderly woman arose and followed by her husband proceeded towards the door. For a moment she stood by my side and looked down at the unknown drunkard. Then she spoke in an aside.

Said she, "I'll say a prayer that he'll go for you." So saying she exited followed by her spouse whilst I returned momentarily to my post behind the counter.

I pretended to busy myself with other business and set about adjusting bottles which needed no adjusting at all. The exercise was meant to distract the attention of the customers away from the drunkard who was now in the deepest sleep. His fitful snores arose like blasphemies to contaminate the drinking area. Running out of things to do I turned on the television. It was near news time and that was sure to be of interest to one and all.

Then the Angelus rang. Its tones silenced every occupant of the premises. All made the sign of the cross and whispered the prayers and aspirations which make up this lovely succession of angelical salutations. Even the snores of the drunkard had subsided. He was silent now, his mouth open, his face twitching. Then without warning of any kind he jumped from his seat and stood to attention. The next thing he did was to cross himself and then to pray with a fervour and sincerity which would do justice to a reverend mother.

He lurched backward and forward all the time but he never fell or budged an inch on his feet. He would sigh now and then as though all his accumulated transgressions were being released at long last. Then preparatory to resuming his slumber, he made the concluding sign of the cross. The many flourishes which accompanied this simple exercise proved to be his undoing.

When his right hand alighted on his forehead, after concluding a sweeping arc of canonical magnificence, I made my move. I darted from behind the counter with the speed of a minnow and seized him by the upraised elbow. It was no bother to spin him around and propel him on to the street without imposing the slightest strain on either one of us.

Where strength and force had failed prayer won the day.

As Tennyson also wrote: "More things are wrought by prayer than this world dreams of."

Corner Boys 3

Wonders will never cease. I thought I'd seen every kind of a corner boy but I suppose it could be said that there are as many kinds of corner boys as there are kinds of corners.

I have been studying this particular corner boy for years and I thought I had him tagged. The other day, however, I had a chance to examine him in isolation. All the other corner boys were absent. The day was not conducive to cornering. It was also early and corner boys do not like to rise before noon. Hence the solitary figure across the road at the corner. In short I would never have noticed the subtle differences in the fellow had it not been for his missing colleagues.

As I watched him I noted that there was a certain amount of unease in his movements. It was as though he were uncertain of himself. Having said this let me also say that there was absolutely no doubt whatsoever in my mind but that he was a genuine, Grade A corner boy. As he looked into space there was that impassive and unmistakeable stare. I'd know it anywhere. If you were to take a corner boy out of his environment and dress him in royal robes and place him on a throne I could always tell that he was a corner boy from his stare. Corner boys spend more time looking into space than they do looking into anything else. This is because there is nothing to be seen in space. No effort whatever is required to look into it. In space there are no distractions so that a corner boy may continue with the vocation of cornering in complete peace.

Sometimes, instead of looking into space, a corner boy will look up and down the street or across the street but he will never see anything because he does not want to see anything. Very few people know it but there is at the back of every corner boy's mind one basic fear and it is that he may one day be called as a witness in a court case. There is, on busy days, always the likelihood of a car crash and during festivals there is the chance of an altercation. Then there are window breakings and attacks by dogs on pedestrians and cyclists. This is why a corner boy is here one minute and gone the next. At the slightest sign of trouble he can vanish faster than a hailstone on a hot griddle. This is his calling and he must never be brought to account for it. The thought of spending a day in court as a witness is frightening. He might actually have to concentrate. Concentration calls for energy and a corner boy is a corner boy in the first place because the expending of energy is anathema to him.

As I watched our friend I could not fully make up my mind what was different about him. Then I grasped it. He did not lean against the corner. He shunned physical contact of any kind with the corner. There was a signpost nearby and now and then he would lean against this.

You may well intervene here and suggest that he was not a real corner boy at all, that he was a signpost boy. No, he was not a signpost boy. He was an authentic corner boy. He could easily ply his trade without the aid of the signpost. Although he did not need the actual corner itself he needed the vicinity of the corner. He could not pursue his vocation anywhere else.

From time to time he would look at his watch as though he were expecting somebody. There would be a worried look on his face. The truth was that he was expecting nobody but he had to give the impression that he was. He had to justify his long vigil at the corner.

Here then was a different corner boy but a certified corner boy nevertheless which begs the question as to how many species of corner boys there are altogether. I reckon if I were to discover a single new type of corner boy every year I would be fulfilling a most valuable role, a role for which I should surely be remembered.

There are more species of corner boys than this world dreams of and this could mean that with the growing urbanisation of the countryside we may wind up with more species than we can classify.

Slave Labour

Slave labour has not ended. As I look out of this upstairs window I observe, emerging from the supermarket across the road, a middle-aged lady dowdily and carelessly dressed, grossly mis-shapen, ghastly of feature, her face faintly tinged with yellow. In her hands she carries two bulging message bags. Her shoulders droop under the weight and her body sways from side to side as she crosses the roadway. She has had to wait for twenty cars to pass before she may safely journey from one side to the other.

Today's motorists are without courtesy or chivalry. There is a persistent drizzle of cloying rain but do you think one of them would stop to allow the overburdened creature to cross? Not on your life.

It amazes me that no priest or missioner has ever sermonised on this lamentable lack of consideration for middle-aged, over-worked women who carry heavy burdens. There are societies for the prevention of cruelty to children and very commendable they are indeed. There are societies for the prevention of cruelty to animals; but there is no society for the prevention of cruelty to middle-aged women and I wonder why.

Meanwhile our friend has succeeded in safely crossing the road and now she comes along Market Street, lumbering like a beast of burden, stopping every so often to draw breath but always pro-ceeding towards that distant spot where her husband has parked his Morris Minor. It is safely hidden somewhere in the outskirts of town because, chances are, it is neither taxed nor insured. If he were to honour these obligations he would be obliged to go without his nightly intake of whiskey and porter and the daily ration of cigarettes. This would never do.

She stops for a moment and surveys the contents of a hardware window. She places the bags gently on the ground. No doubt there are crocks of jam involved and she has to be careful.

It turns out that she has not been investigating the contents of the window at all. She has stopped and placed the bags on the ground at her side in order to turn about so that she can change bags from one hand to the other. It does not matter that the bags are of equal weight or if one barely outweighs the other. What matters is that she believes in the old adage that a change is as good as a rest.

Her husband is nowhere to be seen. It is he who should be carrying the bags for it is he who will be consuming most of the contents or, if not, then himself and the children. It is possible that he is observing her from a safe distance because, you see, she is still not all that familiar with the streets and laneways of the town and there is, therefore, the outside possibility that she might take a wrong turning and go completely astray. I have been witness to similar situations and here is what I have seen happen when a lady with grocery bags went up the street instead of down after coming to the corner of William Street and Market Street which is directly under this window where I write.

When she came to the corner she paused and looked up and down. She was confused. No doubt the weight of the groceries and the dangers of road crossing added to the hundreds of other hazards with which a bustling town presents a mixed-up country woman were more than sufficient to unsettle her. I could see the look of puzzlement on her face and for a moment I was tempted to hurry to her aid. The look of puzzlement changed to determination and it was evident she had made up her mind to go up the street instead of down.

She re-lifted the bags which she had momentarily left on the ground and was about to proceed upwards when she was arrested by a loud protracted whistle. She stopped and looked behind her for the source of the sound and there, standing with his back to the public toilets just outside the cattle mart, was a middle-aged man wearing a cap. No doubt this was her husband.

One whistle had been enough to stop her in her tracks. It was the type of whistle which dog handlers used at sheep trials. Having arrested her with the whistle he lifted his closed left hand and indicated with the thumb that she should take the opposite route to the one which she had chosen. Without a word she turned and proceeded in the direction indicated by her gallant husband.

Canvasser

Around about the time of arrival of the vast majority of cuckoos, which is roughly late April or mid-May, another constant, if not yearly caller will put in its appearance. I refer, of course, to the slow-plodding, dyed-in-the-wool, common or garden Political Canvasser. Easily identified by the solemnity and dignity of its approach, by its tendency to travel in small flocks, its ability to travel diurnally and nocturnally, this harmless passage migrant will disappear completely as soon as the first votes have been cast in the European, Local or General elections.

I confess I have written about this species before but only in the sketchiest of fashions. The truth is that I have, more or less, shied away from the subject because I myself was a canvasser on more than one occasion. I felt that if I wrote at length on the subject it would seem like a betrayal of a trust such as when a former servant snitches on members of the royal family which he once served. I can see it clearly looming across the television screen: "Confessions of a Canvasser" in the *Sunday Contender* or "Former Canvasser Tells All".

Let us now take a fresh look at this business of convassing before the political climate becomes too hot for comments of a comic nature. What exactly is a canvasser? To begin with, he must be a loyal and well-known supporter of any political party. What special qualities are required if a person is to become a canvasser?

Firstly one must be lucky enough or cunning enough to be out of jail at the time of the canvass. Secondly one must be well used to rebuff and thirdly one must be prepared to travel in all kinds of weather.

Let me stress, at this stage, that no two canvassers belonging to the same group should be alike in appearance or temperament. The ideal break-down of any given group of canvassers would read something like this: one conservatively dressed, one sloppily, one dour member and one wise-cracking, one elderly and one teenage, one wealthy and one poor; in short a representative troupe with a certain amount of appeal for everybody. It is well to remember that no two householders are alike and the composition of the canvassing party should always take this into account.

For instance, when the group leader presses the bell on a certain door in a housing estate and receives no answer he will not carry on to the next house. He will press the bell again and again until he is certain that there is nobody there. Now suppose that the door is opened after the third buzz to the bell or after a long series of knocks and that a housewife appears there with hands on hips and ask what in the name of all that's good and holy all the fuss is about.

She accuses the canvassers of waking up the child or, in some cases, her husband. When this happens the most experienced of the canvassers is brought forward. He chides the other canvassers for their lack of sensitivity and then in gentle tones apologises for the behaviour of his colleagues. Slowly but surely he manages to mollify the housewife with varying blandishments and by tendering well-tried cures for gripe and nappy rash.

Then there is the type who answers the door immediately but with such a flood of complaints that the canvassers have no chance to get a word in edgeways. One encounters a voter like this in every twentieth house or so. The thing to do on occasions like these is to produce a member of the party who is related to the candidate if the candidate is not present. He must pretend to listen attentively or even go so far as to make notes of grievances thus allowing the rest of the party to move on to the house next door without seeming to cut short their visit.

Smart as they are and astute as they are, political parties have yet to come up with a Handbook for Canvassers.

In it would be ways and means of handling difficult or hostile householders, standard answers to unanswerable questions, procedures in cases of assault from doughty members of opposing parties, steps to be taken in case of emergency as, for instance, when a baby is suddenly overcome by a fit of convulsions or when a pregnant housewife finds that her hour is come or even when a chimney catches fire because of a draught caused by the opening of two doors at the same time. A Canvassers' Handbook would be a blessing for novice canvassers. It would, of course, have to be an all-party effort. Otherwise there would be such instances of one-upmanship and double dealing that the book would defeat its purpose.

Your dedicated canvasser knocks upon every door whether behind that door lies friend or foe. To pass a door, even that of the most vitriolic member of the opposing party, would be unthinkable.

In every canvass there is generally one door which is dreaded by all. This would be the door of a violent man or woman who hurls abuse, personal and otherwise, upon each and every one of the canvassers. The canvassers always approach this door with caution and trepidation. There is the tendency to knock gently in the hope that the inmates might not hear, but no. The abuser is alert to the most timid of knocks and he answers at once. The thing to do in a case like this is to say that you didn't like to pass by without calling out of respect to the person in question. Then move off without responding no matter how powerful the provocation.

There should be no quips of relief as soon as the group is out of range. There is always the tendency in young canvassers to cock their noses in disdain when they think they are out of harm's reach, just as when a man pursued by a bull thumbs his nose at his pursuer as he nears the safety of the hedge. This is a foolish pastime, either way, but particularly in the case of the canvasser.

I have been present when the canvassed party tiptoed silently after the canvassers, waiting to pounce upon a rash comment. I have seen blows exchanged as a result of an indiscreet remark at the wrong moment. Neither should canvassers give vent to opinions while going through built-up areas. Walls have ears and so have half-opened windows.

The last thing any canvassing party wants is a member who will not play his part. Over the years I have made a study of dodgy canvassers and the worst who comes to mind is he who stands to one side after the bell has been pressed. He flattens himself against the wall at the side of the door in the hope that he won't be seen. He may be just a shy chap who is reluctant to show his face but whatever his motives, he strikes the party being canvassed as a shifty sort of individual. An onlooker could not be blamed either for believing that if one member is shifty all the members of the party must be shifty.

Poorly informed canvassers are no asset to a candidate either. Let us take a situation. The lead canvasser knocks upon a door in a new housing estate. The knock is answered by a strange woman.

"Who is she?" he whispers furiously to one of his troupe. The request is unsuccessfully relayed to the farthest-back member.

Nobody knows who she is. She is a new arrival, of course, which makes identification difficult. Not so with your accomplished canvasser who will have his homework well done beforehand in respect of newcomers to his district.

Another hazard is she who innocently announces that she has no vote in the area after the canvassers have expended valuable time and energy on her. Again your astute canvasser who has properly researched his register will be well aware that she has no vote and will only make a perfunctory stop before moving on to more rewarding pastures.

These are but a few of the hazards facing canvassers and I hope it will now be appreciated that one does not become a successful canvasser overnight. In constituencies where neck and neck contests are traditional the accomplished canvasser can often shade the issue while an incompetent one can cost the candidate his seat.

A Wake-Room Saga

At a wake recently I was offered a glass of whiskey which I gladly accepted. Normally I would forego whiskey by day but I was suffering from a cold in the stomach and tradition tells us that a small quantity of spirits, judiciously taken, has been known to cope successfully with the pangs that accompany such abdominal visitations.

Clutching my whiskey I sought out a quiet place in the kitchen next to the wake-room. It would have been a breach of wake-room protocol to swallow the whiskey at once and depart the scene. Luckily I happened upon a vacant corner with standing room for one only. At either side of me sat dour, disapproving damsels of advanced ages, dour because there was no room for them in the overcrowded wake-room and disapproving because others seemed to be enjoying themselves.

There are still to be found, in town and country, women who

cannot bear to be separated from corpses. It is not that they are inclined towards morbidity or that they have a fascination with the dead. It is, purely and simply, that the wake-room is where the action is. Here the corpse is laid out with loving care, with the traditional prayer book propping up the chin and rosary beads entwined around bloodless hands. Here is where the comings and goings are, where strangers and neighbours alike may be studied at length when they kneel to pray by the side of the corpse.

Also at the door of the wake-room drinks are given around with greater regularity than any other part of the house. As I leaned comfortably against the walls of my corner, minding my own business, sipping my whiskey and endeavouring with all my faculties to convey to the public at large the sorrowful disposition of a sincere mourner, I noticed that I was under surveillance by a tall man with a thin nose and an extremely long jaw.

I sensed, from long and painful experience, that the fellow had a story to tell and since I was the only person in the kitchen who might fairly be described as a professional purveyor of stories I guessed that he was contemplating a visit. The fact that a corpse was on public display in an adjoining room was of no consequence to him. He had a tale to tell, an oft-told tale for sure and certain, and he was going to unload this tale were he felt it would do the most good.

Clutching my whiskey I looked around for an avenue of escape but there was none. The only exit was manned by the would-be storyteller. Then I indulged in a truly hypocritical exercise. I closed my eyes and pretended that I was praying. In fact I was in the act of silently reciting prayers but they were not for the repose of the soul of the faithful departed. They were solely intended for my own self preservation. I couldn't have luck. I suddenly felt a nudge and there he was, endeavouring to crowd two of us into a corner where there was only room for one.

"I must tell you a story," he said and without as much as by your leave he opened with the first chapter of a rambling saga which I had heard many a time before.

In the hands of a lively raconteur or natural storyteller the tale could have been told in two minutes or less but this buffoon insisted in going beyond his brief at every possible opportunity.

I coughed politely when a break in the epic presented itself.

"I heard it before," I informed him. He kept going, however.

"I heard it before," I repeated the protest with more emphasis.

"That's a pity," he said and at once he launched into a torrent of words about the state of the country, the future of the country, the economy and what have you. He made no sense whatsoever. In desperation I handed him my whiskey as earnest.

"Hold that," I said, "until I come back from the toilet." He did so with pleasure, never dreaming that I would forfeit a perfectly good glass of whiskey rather than subject myself to further punishment.

Outside I hid myself among several solid countrymen at the gable end of the house. In a matter of moments a second glass of whiskey was placed in my hand. The men about me lifted their glasses in silent commemoration.

I thought of the storyteller waiting inside. Shakespeare had his likes well tagged. Remember *The Merchant of Venice*:

> Gratiano speaks an infinite deal of nothing.
> More than any man in all Venice.
> His reasons are as two grains of wheat
> Hid in two bushels of chaff.
> You shall seek all day ere you find them
> And when you have them they are not worth
> The search.

Close That Door

It is twenty years now since I first wrote about the opening and closing of doors. On that occasion I dealt with the subject in a facetious fashion but now, having become embittered at the injustice of doors left open carelessly and deliberately, I propose to take a harsher look at this contentious subject.

One night during the recent cold spell the door of these very licensed premises where I am at present in residence was left open seven times. Seven times the warm interior was chilled by the heedless and callous lack of concern which is the hallmark of all those villainous and selfish wretches who are always ready to open a door but are never prepared to close it.

By comparison with these unconvicted criminals who never close or only partly close doors the majority of those unfortunates who are presently incarcerated could well be said to be innocent. Which is worse I ask you: allowing a door to remain ajar in cold weather or the misappropriation of a few pounds to keep body and soul together? I would go so far as to say that if you were to scour the dungeons of the universe you would not find the equals of the ruffians who subject their fellow humans to dangerous draughts and sudden falls in temperature.

I was once visited by the victim of a chronic door criminal. There he had been sitting by his fire when his brother-in-law entered and announced that he needed the loan of £120 to pay the insurance on his car. He sat for a while near the fire explaining his case. Finally to get rid of him our friend wrote a cheque for the amount and saw the beggar out only to discover to his horror that the kitchen door had not been properly closed. As a result he contracted a vicious pain on his right shoulder and could not look either sideways or behind him for several weeks.

Calling for a whiskey he vented his fury on his brother-in-law.

"I'll tell you something now," he said, "and it comes from the heart." So saying he swallowed his whiskey and spoke as follows.

Said he, "If I had my way I would execute one in four of these offensive knaves."

"You mean one in every four of brother-in-laws or one in every four of ordinary in-laws?" I asked.

"Neither," he said, "for I believe that there are more good in-laws than bad. I also believe that bad in-laws eventually punish themselves. Therefore, I will leave in-laws alone. No my friend, the people to whom I refer are those who do not fully close doors behind them. Of these I would cheerfully shoot, hang, drown or dismember one in every four. I would not do it as an act of revenge. I would do it in good faith as a deterrent and if a man were to come to me in the morning and suggest that these criminals be beheaded I would gladly provide him with spikes on which to exhibit the trunkless heads on the approaches to places of worship and entertainment."

Seriously speaking, if I were asked to recommend a suitable punishment for men and women who do not close doors behind them I would opt for a mandatory prison sentence of one month. Nowhere does a man become more conscious of closed doors than in prison. The door is all that confines him. He can scale walls but he cannot draw back outside bolts.

Recently at the height of the inclement weather when breezes and draughts were chillingly reinforced by the penetrating cold of snow a customer of mine allowed the door to remain open behind him three nights in a row. When the cold came in the heat went out. The other customers shivered and I was forced to suspend the culprit. He showed no concern at all for the other patrons, expecially for the elderly who cannot cope with the cold as well as the middle-aged and the young. I actually heard the following indictment of the door criminal from a pious client of seventy-seven.

Said he with a venom, "The bastard should be hung, drawn and quartered."

"No! No! No!" his wife contradicted. "He should be made stand in a draught for a year."

Let these few words, therefore, serve as a warning to all those thoughtless perverts who do not close doors behind them. As you sow so shall you reap and he that closeth not the door shall knock in vain and he shall linger at the portals of eternity but he that closeth the door shall knock but once and he shall be heard and it shall be opened.

Jack Scoodle

Reading about how prone great football stars are to injuries I was reminded of another sportsman, at a far lower level, who suffered one major injury which changed the whole course of his life.

Unlike injury-prone athletes you could be hitting and kicking this man for a month of Sundays and you wouldn't draw a drop of blood or leave a mark on him. We shall call him Jack Scoodle for the good reason that there are no Scoodles in this part of the world.

Jack played at full forward for the Wagnahoola junior football team and it was said of him that he permanently incapacitated more of his own team than he did the opposition. In those days full forwards were chosen for their strength and height rather than for their football skill or IQ.

At school Jack Scoodle was a dunce. Some said he was retarded but this was not strictly true. Jack wasn't a real fool. He was never late for his meals. As he grew up his parents began to fear for his future. They apprenticed him to a number of trades with disastrous results. They got him a job as a counter hand, an assistant to a paper hanger, an apprentice to a whitewasher and countless other positions. In the end he wound up with a pick and shovel which he could put to tolerable use provided there was somebody peering over his shoulder from start to finish. On his own he had few peers as a pipe buster and shovel breaker.

Then came the junior league and he was selected as usual at full forward. In the opening moments a lobbing ball came into the square. Jack Scoodle jumped high, drew a clenched fist at the ball, missed but succeeded in rendering both goalie and fullback unconscious. With nobody to impede its progress the ball ended up in the back of the net.

When the fullback and goalie came around they were somewhat shaken with the result that they were taken off and replaced by two brothers known to be the most outstanding blackguards that part of the world had ever produced. So perverse were their natures that when they could find nobody else to beat they beat one another and when they tired of that they were not beyond drawing playful clouts at their father and mother.

They were placed at full back and goal respectively and when the next high ball came lobbing into the square they ignored its progress altogether and devoted their combined attention to the full forward, your friend and mine, Jack Scoodle.

Scoodle stood with his face towards the heavens awaiting the most appropriate moment to jump and maybe bang the ball into the net for a second goal. As soon as his attention was totally committed to the dropping ball the older of the brothers struck Jack Scoodle on the extremity of the jaw. Jack staggered and fell and when he showed signs of rising the younger brother promptly kicked him into the side of the head.

Jack Scoodle lay inert. The ball had gone harmlessly wide and the referee admonished the brothers for carrying things a bit too far.

Time passed and Jack Scoodle spent several weeks hovering between life and death. Eventually he recovered. He sat up in his hospital bed and demanded the daily papers, something he had never before done. Although previously illiterate he read them from cover to cover thereby amazing all his friends and relations. When he left hospital he built a new house for his mother and father after which he announced that he would be leaving for England to make his fortune.

"Why not!" the neighbours exclaimed. "Did he not read the papers and did he not build a house?"

In England he became a millionaire in no time at all. He never played football thereafter and wouldn't he be the pure fool if he had. The kick in the head was the making of him and he had enough newly acquired brains to deduce that if he played football again and got a second kick in the head he might very well be reduced to his former incapacitated state.

Townies

Dan Paddy Andy O'Sullivan, the great Irish matchmaker, had no time for townies. The reason was that a young female neighbour of his was once taken down by one.

"A fine slip of a girl she was to be sure," Dan told us. "You'd look around on the road after her and there was many a green gorsoon that guided his donkey into a ditch after she passing."

Anyhow she happened to fall in love with a townie and according to Dan Paddy Andy he had all the characteristics of your true townie. There were his low shoes or slippers as country folk called them in those days. Then the good-for-nothing apparently wore a collar and tie on a continuing basis without ever having earned the right to sport same. It might not have been too bad if he was a schoolteacher or an insurance agent or a warble fly inspector but the fellow was none of these things. His chief sources of income were his father's and mother's pensions and, of course, the weekly dole which he unfailingly drew from the local unemployment exchange.

Dan Paddy Andy would shake his head in horror as he outlined the remainder of the townie's failings.

"Rumour has it," said Dan, "that the imposter shaves every day and is never without a crease in his hair or his trousers whether the day is Sunday or Monday."

On top of that he was not above using stink. At least Dan said he used it. Stink in this instance would be after-shave lotion, a rarity of rarities at the time. In fact the only time after-shave lotion was smelled in country places was when some emigrant returned from America.

On top of all this the townie in question used hair oil the seven days of the week but worst of all he carried a nail file in an inside pocket. This last was felt to be the be-all and end-all of blackguardism. Nail files were all right for film stars but for a townie with no job and a deep dislike of jobs it was felt that he was outstepping himself.

In addition to all this he wore white socks, was never done whistling day or night and was, according to Dan, "a hoor for cheek-to-cheek dancin'."

Dan advised the girl to have nothing to do with this particular townie and when that failed he went to the girl's parents.

"There are some townies and they're not too bad," Dan explained, "townies that will do an honest week's work and take off their caps to a priest the same as ourselves but this buck I'm talkin' about is the worst kind of townie. He won't work and he won't look for work."

The parents promised to do what they could but they were old and all their importuning fell on deaf ears. Other sources claimed that this townie was an indoor man by day and an outdoor man by night which simply meant that he liked to spend the day in front of the fire and the night carousing. Fond as he was of the fire he would never go to the bog to cut the winter's supply of fuel. He allowed his father and mother to cut and foot the turf.

In the end the poor country girl married him and he took her to live with his father and mother. The pair lived unhappily together although, fortunately, not ever after. Herself and her father-in-law and mother-in-law worked their fingers to the bones to keep the wretch in drink and cigarettes and when he arrived home from the pub at night there would be bedlam if there wasn't a plate of sausages or mutton cutlets awaiting him. He always dressed like a dandy while his mother and his wife slunk from house to church and back in the blackest of black shawls.

Luckily he died after about ten years from a disease of the liver and after a decent interval his widow returned to her home in the Stacks Mountains. In due course Dan Paddy Andy went matchmaking for her and found for her, not far from the town of Killarney, a small farmer. This man was no gorsoon but he was an artist with spade and shovel. He made a good husband and the pair had several children.

I need hardly add that they lived happily ever after. Years after Dan Paddy Andy met her at the fair of Puck and she told him that her only regret was that she hadn't listened to him in the first place.

"Well," Dan said, "you listened to your heart and there's no harm in that if the man's any use."

A Magnanimous Man

The year was nineteen forty-six. It was the year that white flour began to reappear and it was the year that ten leading Nazi war criminals were hanged. It was also the year that Italy proclaimed itself a republic and last but not least it was the year that Jackeen Jollop returned home from England after having spent the final year of the war working in a munitions factory. Jackeen Jollop is not his real name but we will adhere to it for the duration of our narrative in order to protect the innocent as the saying goes.

Although he had only spent a year in England Jackeen had acquired a Cockney accent or what passed for a Cockney accent. He knew everything. He was never stuck for an answer. He knew Field Marshal Montgomery well. He used to call Jackeen by his first name whenever they met in the Elephant and Acorn which happened to be Jackeen's local.

"Call me Mont," he had told Jackeen, "and don't let me hear no more of this Field Marshal clatter."

Jackeen knew Sir Gordon Richards although he was only plain Gordon at that time. Still Jackeen was big enough to include him in his circle of cronies.

"Do you know who was a helluva nice bloke?" Jackeen would recall when he had a few pints of stout under his belt.

"Who was that?" we would ask.

"Eisenhower," Jackeen would come back at once. Apparently Jackeen was eating out one night in the Goosander Grill when who should pop in but Eisenhower and some other general.

Eisenhower ordered a fillet steak and his friend ordered the same. At the time Jackeen was awaiting an order of rook pie, this being an unrationed commodity during the war.

"Rooks is awright," Jackeen used to say, "once you get used to the blighters." Anyway it transpired that Eisenhower was dissatisfied with his steak and told the waiter so in no uncertain terms.

"I'm danged," said Eisenhower, "if this ain't horsemeat."

"Well," said the waiter, who according to Jackeen was a forward sort of a fellow and a rogue to boot, "when you ordered the steak you didn't say whether it was cowmeat or horsemeat you wanted."

"That will do you," Jackeen intervened. The waiter was about to make a smart remark but upon beholding Jackeen's steely eyes though better of it.

"Hand me over that horsemeat," Jackeen said, "and you can give Ike my rook pie."

"Who is this guy?" Ike asked. Jackeen introduced himself and when Ike heard he was from North Kerry he asked him how the Kerry team was faring in the football championship.

"Nicer than Ike you just could not meet," Jackeen told us. Apparently he also invited Jackeen to spend a holiday in the States but Jackeen declined on the grounds that he might only insult Charlie Chaplin who had, the year before, also invited him to the States.

"You just can't make fish of one and fowl of the other," Jackeen explained.

Then we found ourselves in Dublin in the September of nineteen forty-six. The All-Ireland football final had just concluded at Croke Park. We had a few pounds in our pockets from our summer labours so we decided to invest in one decent meal in the best hotel we could find.

The menus were handed round and we all waited for Jackeen to order.

"There's horsemeat on it," said a wag.

"Where?" Jackeen asked.

"Look," said the wag and he pointed his finger at the hors d'oeuvres.

"Horses' dovaries," said Jackeen smacking his lips. "I often ate 'em over."

Just for the heck of it we all said we'd chance the horses' dovaries. Eventually they arrived. When Jackeen's plate was placed in front of him he nearly choked with disgust. On the plate was egg mayonnaise, chopped onion, sliced tomato and two sardines.

"Here, mate!" he called to the waiter and he lifted one of the sardines for the fellow's benefit.

"What's wrong?" the waiter asked politely.

"What's wrong!" Jackeen fumed. "Just tell me what part of a horse is a sardine?" he shouted. "You won't fool me so easily. I been over, mate, and I knows horses' dovaries from sardines."

We all applauded and we persuaded Jackeen to forgive the waiter who obviously didn't know any better the poor fellow. It was plain that he had never been over.

"Awright, awright," Jackeen conceded, "we all makes mistakes."

No wonder this magnanimous man was befriended by Eisenhower, Charlie Chaplin, Sir Gordon Richards and Field Marshal Montgomery.

Kerry Nick-Names

"Get out, you hoorin' gander," I heard the angry command in a south Kerry public house on the evening of a summer's day many years ago. The remark was addressed to an amiable but drunken countryman who had ordered a half pint of stout from the proprietor. The countryman's amiability vanished at once and was replaced by a rampant hostility towards the wretch who would compare him with the male of the common goose.

In my company at the time was an elderly schoolmaster, well-versed in local history and regarded by one and all in that rustic community as the ultimate redress in any dispute.

"Do not take it to heart," he said to the man who had been linked with ganders as he forcibly held him by the arm lest he lay hands on the proprietor.

"But he called me a hoorin' gander," the poor fellow whose name was Mulligan pouted.

"And not without reason," said the schoolmaster, "for your paternal grandfather was a man who distributed fat ganders every Christmas amid the poor of the parish and was thus called the Gander Mulligan."

Greatly heartened the descendant of the Gander Mulligan approached the man behind the counter and spoke to him as me was Ganders and all that comes after me will be Ganders with the help of God. We're known all over the world and the schoolmaster here tells me too that in Newfoundland there's an airport called after us."

So saying he made for the door, threw back his head and gave the distinct impression that he was used to drinking in better places. The moral here, of course, is that we should make light of our every soubriquet.

We have, all of us, heard the Gaelic expression Tadhg an dá Thaobh. The nickname is frequently applied to men who take two sides. In every one of us is a goodly sprinkling of Tadhg an dá Thaobh and this is clearly illustrated at election times when we promise more than one person that we will vote for them. Ninety-nine percent of us do this and we must not be blamed because when the election is over we must resume normal relationships. It is therefore no shame then to be called a Tadhg an dá Thaobh.

Now let us take the case of the Boozer Muldoon, a legendary character who once lived near Ballybunion in North Kerry. Naturally his descendants, all now deceased, were also known as the Boozer Muldoons. They took a rather dim view of this insalubrious soubriquet and there were many altercations and instances of outright assault whenever the name Boozer was applied.

Again it was a schoolmaster who put an end to the numerous wrangles concerning the nickname. The occasion was the fifteenth of August.

Ballybunion when I was a gorsoon was a notorious place for settling old scores on the famous pattern day and there were instances of serious injury when things got out of hand. Anyway the Boozer Muldoon, an otherwise most abstemious individual, decided to celebrate the pattern.

He took a drink or two in several hostelries and found the outing highly beneficial until somebody inadvertently addressed him as the Boozer Muldoon. Actually the man who used the term did so in good faith for upon beholding the Boozer he simply said, "Will you have a drink, Boozer?"

To which the Boozer replied, "How dare you call me Boozer, you pratey-snapping reject of a mermaid's litter."

With that he went about wading into his tormentor when he was seized by a middle-aged schoolmaster who happened to be present on the occasion.

"Why are you assaulting this man?" asked the schoolmaster.

"Because he called me Boozer," said the Boozer Muldoon.

"And why wouldn't he call you Boozer," admonished the schoolmaster, "when your father before you was a Boozer?"

At this the Boozer Muldoon bridled but not for long.

"The reason your father was called the Boozer," said the schoolmaster, "was because he would sit far-in by his father's hearth and listen for the distant boozing of Black and Tan lorries. Upon hearing same he would risk life and limb until he located local members of the Flying Column and inform them of the presence of the enemy."

At this the Boozer Muldoon swelled up with pride and indicated to the barmaid that free drink was to be given to the man who addressed him as the Boozer and to the schoolmaster who notified him of his proud heritage. The moral is this. However belittling your nickname there may be more to you than you think.

Honeymooners

"Beware of all enterprises that require new clothes."

So spake David Henry Thoreau, the great American philosopher.

One enterprise which requires new clothes is the sacrament of marriage. It also requires a number of other things but let us begin with the required raiment. Nowadays it is not uncommon to see a young gentleman pronounce the two words of eternal acceptance wearing a suit which owes its freshness and creases to the local dry cleaners. This is fine if he cannot afford a new suit but I very much fear that the opposite is often the case.

New clothes provide a sense of occasion although I believe I would be prepared to forgive a man who has already embarked upon the marriage stakes a number of times previously. Obviously he does not take marriage seriously and should not, therefore, himself be taken seriously.

When Thoreau tells us that we should beware of all enterprises that require new clothes he is warning us about marriage and, in fact, is asking us to look before weleap.While he doesn't actually council long courtships in so many words the suggestion is nevertheless there. He does not tell us to avoid occasions which require new clothes. He merely tells usto be on our guard and not to take such occasions lightly.

Some men, particularly defendants, dress in spotless new suits complete with shining shirts and sombre ties when they are obliged to go to a court of law. I am not saying that judges or juries will be swayed by new clothes. What I am saying is that they will not be swayed by slack or indifferent dress.

It is, however, with marriage that we should concern ourselves at this present time. A man who marries in a hurry will not have had the time to spare up for a new suit. Therefore, it is a wise man who does not marry in a hurry for he shall have new clothes and new shoes and all. He shall be spick and he shall be span and neither shall he have holes in his socks as I have seen in some recent marriages.

I remember during the early days of these very licensed premises over which I presently strive to entertain and enlighten my readers there would be a regular spate of honeymooners prior to the Shrovetide period. They still come and I hope they will continue to come for years yet but they are not nearly as plentiful as they used to be.

You could recognise them immediately from the newness of their apparel. They had neither the guile nor the experience to change out of their new clothes so that it was easy to guess why they were all dressed up. It was also possible, I must concede, to mistake a long married couple who might only have been attending a wedding for a newly married pair. The former would also be wearing new clothes because of their respect and regard for the sacrament which still happily bound them together.

However, there were certain minor aspects of the picture which, accumulated, served to confirm the suspicion that we were being presented with anauthentic newly married couple. The groom generally sported a fresh haircut and in those days barbers really cut hair. There was little styling. The idea was to remove the hair from the head without making the subject look bald. Fine if he looked bare since this was the object of the exercise. As well as having his hair freshly cut the groom would also have a pronounced crease running down the side of the head, a head which still bore a shine from the excessive hair oil applied that very morning or even the day before.

Another weighty piece of evidence was the new white shirt sported by the groom and if this wasn't enough there was the new tie, the knot of which had slipped so that it had drifted downwards altogether from its rightful place in front of the collar button.

Another piece of evidence, particularly if he were a farmer, was the squeak from his new shoes. This was always regarded as the most conclusive evidence of all. Your cunning townie or city slicker would have made sure beforehand to change his shoes if they squeaked but your naive countryman, naive only in this respect, was a dead give-away because of his outspoken footwear.

There were other things. If you happened to glance at his hands you would see that his nails had been cut to the bone, especially for the occasion. There would be a crease on his trousers capable of cutting through a pound of butter. Often he would be the embarrassed proprietor of a brand new wallet. All his money was kept here and every now and then his hand would stray to his breast pocket to make sure that it was still there. He would also sit very close to his brand new bride who would sit silently and demurely taking in her new surroundings, as Shakespeare said, with an easy span.

She would be the cuter of the two in more ways than looks and would have been extremely difficult to identify but for the proximity of her newly taken mate who was unmistakeably new to the role. There were small clues, however, by which she might be authenticated in the event of her partner revealing nothing.

Brides, until recent times, would very often wear navy blue costumes when leaving the wedding festivities with their new consorts. A white blouse was also an outstanding feature of her honeymoon habiliments whilst it would also be obvious that her hair had been recently permed. At that time few honeymooners went abroad where total anonymity was guaranteed and where the hot sun militated against the wearing of any sort of official or traditional costume.

The bride would also be wearing new high-heeled shoes which, believe it or not, were frequently reviled as immoral by certain matrons of the period. There was even a derogatory song entitled "The High-Heeled Shoes."

Another give-away was the last drink of the female. While the groom contented himself with a few half whiskies and maybe a half pint or two of stout the bride would nearly always venture to sherry or port from the customary mineral for the final drink of the night.

Also she would be at pains from the moment of entry to the moment of departure to give the impression that nothing out of the ordinary was about to happen that night. In fact, she sat so primly and correctly that the impression was given that the consummation of the marriage was the farthest thought from her head. In most cases I can still tell when a honeymoon couple enter the premises. I must confess, however, that there are these days many couples who seem to have been married for years.

Beware of all enterprises that require new clothes! Marriage really is about the only enterprise that still calls for new clothes. I am happy to be able to report that all the couples who visited these premises over the years have returned again and again to prove Thoreau right. In wearing new clothes, however stilted it made them appear to others, they were taking their obligations seriously. I am absolutely certain that all such marriages survived all obstacles.

The preparation was there and the commitment was there. There were long courtships and if some thought them too long the marriages that emerged from them were durable and happy. Not only were those couples of yesterday married but they were seen to be married as well and there's never anything to be ashamed of about that.

Corner Boys 4

The other morning as I sat looking aimlessly out of my window awaiting the arrival of the day's first corner boy I said to the missus who happened to be standing behind me, "I don't know what I'll write about."

"Write about corner boys," she said just as one of these intrepid denizens of the downtown scene took up his position at the corner nearest and dearest to me.

"I've said all there is to be said about corner boys," I told the missus but just after I had spoken I noticed a facet of the corner boy's makeup which had escaped me up until this time.

Shortly after he had taken up his position he stamped his feet proprietorially, thrust his hands deep into his pockets, removed himself from the corner proper to the tune of about three feet, flexed himself and stamped his feet a second time. It was easy to see that he was establishing proprietorship but there was something I had not noticed before. There was in his whole presentation a fierce desire to be seen. He strutted for several yards at either side of the corner as though he were staking a claim but the reality was that he was showing himself off, exhibiting his right to self expression and saying, as it were, to the world, "I am here. Behold me maintaining my corner. Take note of me and beware."

After a period of preening and strutting which lasted for about five minutes he turned his attention to passers-by and heard them out briefly before returning to lend his support to the corner by leaning against it with his buttocks and back alternately. Then he stepped forward once more and stood his ground firmly in the centre of the street whilst ladies with fully-laden message bags were obliged to change their tack so as to avoid bumping into him. They made no protest either by word or deed and this recognition of the corner boy's right to impede them served to establish more fully the corner boy's right to exhibit himself for the benefit of all those who might be unaware of his presence.

It is the God-given right of corner boys to obstruct all passers-by regardless of their gender or importance. A corner boy will never deliberately bump into a pedestrian but he will so position himself that it will always behove those who pass by to take evasive action so as to avert a collision.

It is merely the corner boy's way of affirming his immovability by intimating to all and sundry that they pass by on sufferance. Whilst I have never seen a corner boy use physical force to put pedestrians in their place his disposition suggests that the likelihood is always there.

I often think too that corner boys avail of corners to keep pedestrians on the move. There is a tendency in each of us to stop at corners, to look up and down and up again before crossing the road but there is the added danger that we may needlessly dawdle because the corner is a vantage point from which several areas may be viewed at the same time. It is a natural stopping place like an oasis or ford.

It is when this happens that the corner boy shows himself at his most intimidatory. His eyes flash, his countenance grows grim and his whole body tenses. His demeanour would seem to say, "Move along there or I'll move you myself." I daresay this could be called corner-boy presence.

It is a good thing the corner boy is there. Women in particular tend to cause consternation at corners by standing to look here, there and everywhere and by availing of the respite to change a grocery bag from one hand to the other or by simply utilising an encounter with another female to open a long conversation, thereby cluttering a corner so that people have to avail of the roadway to get to their destination. An aggressive corner-boy will quickly put an end to this irrelevant but obstructive gibberish by simply placing himself between the women in question so that conversation becomes impossible. Men are more secretive and tend to move away from corners to unfrequented spaces where privacy assures the confidentiality of their exchanges.

This then is a facet of the corner boy's character which we overlooked until this time. It should serve to remind us that there is no end to the points which contribute to the makeup of any given human being. So vast and complex is the composition of the most insignificant of our fellows that it could well be said that man is infinite in his capacity to keep on revealing chapter after chapter of the never-ending story of his lifestyle.

Distorted Outlooks

I have long believed that geographical upheavals such as the introduction of one-way streets and no-entry signs can be the cause of changed or distorted outlooks in those people whose everyday movements are restricted or altered by the afore-mentioned transmogrifications. Things are never the same afterwards. Alter one thing in a town and you alter everything.

At this moment as I write I can see below me through my magic window the still bewildered faces of motorists who have only just become aware of the fact that they now can drive only in one direction and not all over the place as before. Listowel is a new town in more ways than one since the introduction of the new traffic laws. Gone are the jams and the hold-ups and all are agreed that the new system is an unqualified success.

Alas there is the question of the distorted outlooks. In this particular case it is manifested in reports of a series of wildly improbable sexual exploits circulating through the various gossip stations at the moment. It is several years now since Listowel was last visited by such outrageous fables of debauch.

The last time the fantasies concerned themselves with wife-swapping. I must say here, of course, that no town worth its salt is free from the occasional sexual deviation as imagined by the established gossips who retail the news to mirage-indentured, reverie-starved clients who, in turn, freely embellish all they have been told.

There is always a market for dirty stories about innocent people. The wilder and more spurious the sexual extravaganzas the better. The average lives of these outbreaks is short like a forest fire or an ass's gallop. They have, therefore, to be far above the pedestrian if they are to make any sort of lasting impact. Ordinary scandal such as rape and incest do not quite fit the bill. Something more bizarre is needed.

I am convinced, as indeed are many of the sages who frequent my hostelry, that the change in the town's traffic laws is directly responsible.

The tragedy is that word of the unlikely doings in Listowel has spread far afield and recently while in Killarney I was confronted with the sexual shenanigans allegedly taking place in my beloved town. What does one say when ones native place is thus impeached? An emphatic denial only succeeds in convincing the accuser that his charges are true whereas a half-hearted denial is even worse. The accuser is convinced either way. Should one say nothing? This would be uncivil and to add the sin of incivility to all the other sins of which the town stands accused would be to do further damage.

To crown all an anonymous rhymer has composed a sort of dirge about the death of the town's morals. I have only heard it second-hand and a puerile effort it is I must say. I doubt if it will catch on. I can recall no lampoon about the town or its people which did. This particular one comes in unrhyming trochaic tetrameter as in Longfellow's "Hiawatha". There the resemblance ends.

The present scandalous spate of rumours shows no sign of abating at the time of writing. We must wait, alas, until some calamity befalls a luckless soul or souls from some other area.

Sorry. I said earlier that I could recall no lampoon on Listowel that lasted. One comes to mind written over sixty years ago by a balladmaker called Paddy Drury. Drury was illiterate and had to go to bed when composing. With the clothes pulled over his head he would commit the freshly made lines to memory. Anyway here is what he had to say about the town of Listowel:

Abbeyfeale for flour and meal,
Cahirmee for horses.
The Convent Cross for pitch and toss,
And Listowel for kiss me arse.

The Lord be good to Paddy Drury. He was also hard on his native Knockanure:

Knockanure both mean and poor,
A church without a steeple,
With bitches and hoors looking over halfdoors,
Criticisin' dacent people.

100

Anyway that's the position in Listowel at the present time. I am personally convinced that as soon as the people become accustomed to the new traffic regulations the sex gossip will stop.

Called Off

I could write about Gaelic football from one end of the day to the other but not, however, about the finer points of the game or the reasons why matches are won and lost. I will leave this to sports journalists whose detachment is beyond question and who are so trained that partisanship plays no part whatsoever in their disposition towards tense encounters. My function is to record the sublime and the ridiculous and comment on the peculiar and the unusual in between. In my time I have written about the long white varicosed legs of junior football fullbacks, about the rotundity of corner forwards, hard, roundy and knacky as Castlegregory onions and about full forwards who, through their very awkwardness, are more of an asset to the opposition than to their own.

I could go on and on and on but instead I will treat with the time a drunken player of my acquaintance and of my own football heyday was signalled by a sideline mentor and informed by a series of emphasised hand signals that his services were no longer required and that the said mentor would be obliged if the player in question were to remove himself at once from the field of play and take up his position on the substitutes' bench where a soberer and more eager youth was waiting to enter the fray.

All the drunken player did, by way of answer, was to pull up his already pulled-up socks, cock his head in the air and arch his indignant rump in the general direction of the man who would dispense with his services before running off to the farthest corner of the field where the pleas of the mentors and selectors alike would be rendered useless by sheer distance. He reminded me of nothing but a capricious donkey stallion who has been alerted in his morning pasture by the sight of reins and winkers in the hands of a green youth who would harness him for the bog.

Times were then different, of course. Authority was inconsistent, to say the least, and if the man called off was physically stronger than the man who wanted him off, it goes without saying that the drunkard was always allowed to finish the game without further harrassment.

Different if it was a spindly player renowed for his temerity. He might, with impunity, be addressed as follows: "Come off, you hoor, don't I tear the heart out of you!"

Towards the end of my playing days I was myself called off but in my case I greeted the request with relief and delight rather than with resentment and anger for, at the age of thirty-six, I had just been bested in a lengthy buckle with a teenage back so that being told to lie down was a gesture of compassion rather than chastisement. Purely and simply my knees had given out and if I hadn't been called off I would have collapsed from pure exhaustion.

I am aware that there are many players who would prefer to be sent off than called off. The humiliation and degradation of what is believed in Gaelic circles to be the longest and loneliest sports journey in the world, i.e., from field of play to sideline, is more than most players can stomach and, paradoxically, it was regarded to be more sporting to strike an opposing player with a clenched fist and be sent off than to be called off for doing nothing at all.

Sometimes to save a player embarrassment when he was selected for the sideline an official or two would hurry to where he had prostrated himself, feigning the anguish of mortal injury by writhing and groaning on the ground. Between them they would lift him and, supporting him between them, would half-carry, half-drag him to the sideline where others would lovingly lay him out, maybe to pull his leg to counteract cramp or chafe his palms to bring back circulation while feverish, whispered releases were thrown backwards to sceptical onlookers that it was the collarbone or the cartilage or an acute attack of common cramp.

I remember once to see a savage altercation between a called-off player and a sideliner: "Lie down," shouted the sideliner after the player in question had kicked seven wides in a row.

"Make me," said the kicker of wides. In a matter of seconds, they were at it hammer and tongs but the upshot of the ruction was that the player was allowed to stay on because his physical master was not to be found among the sideliners.

Let those who have never been called off beware. Sooner or later it falls to the lot of every footballer. My advice is to accept the inevitable with good grace. It is no shame and, but for a willingness to serve beyond one's normal time and the ultimate bid to win footballing glory, the occasion would not have arisen. Respond at once when called for, in so doing, you will save yourself further disgrace and even more quickly than the crawling caterpillar is transformed into a butterfly, the aspiring sub is transformed into a player. This is, after all, what substitutes are for, i.e., to be called on when others are called off and is it not the very essence of logic to assert that if nobody was ever called off nobody would ever be called on?

Many who are called off never forgive the men who did the calling and here they may be putting a rope around the neck of an innocent man for, as often as not, the caller is simply acting upon a decision reached by the selectors as a whole. Often too the caller is chosen to do the dirty work because other selectors may well want friends or relations of their own on the team. It could be said that it is these faceless scoundrels who sign the death warrant but that it is the unfortunate caller-offer who is made to put on the black cap.

Then there was the cousin of mine who, because he was called off during the dying moments of a local final, did not appear in his favourite public house for several months so ignominious was he made to feel. In time he attained to his normal drinking capacity but he never pulled a jersey over his head thereafter. Often, in his cups, he would shake his head and speak to himself. Always he made the same statement: "Call me anything," he would say, "but don't call me off."

Now let us look at the real villian of the piece.

Sometimes when the star player of a side was delayed by accident or simply through his own vanity a Sooner was put in his place until he showed up. In Gaelic football a Sooner is a man who would sooner be presented with a soft ball from a colleague than make the effort to win the ball himself. He was a player who was repeatedly tried and found wanting but these reverses never did anything to cull his aspirations. Consequently when he was temporarily selected his heart soared. The villainy surfaced when the star arrived and hastily togged out.

The man who was keeping his seat warm, as it were, was notified that his time was at hand and that he should be gearing himself for the journey to the sideline. He did the very opposite. He moved as far from the sideline in question as was physically possible and, despite repeated entreaties, followed by threats of savage reprisal, he refused to come off the field. The longer he stayed on the less chance his team had of winning.

On this account, he was exhorted by supporters of the opposing team to stay where he was. He assumed that this was general approbation and cocked his snoot at those who would have him on the sideline. Very often, the mentors would be forced to wait until the half-time whistle was blown before they succeeded in convincing him that he was a usurper. Generally, a well-aimed, forceful kick in the seat of his togs was necessary but there were times when he was obliged to run for his life out of the grounds by the man for whom he over-deputised.

The Story of Oisín

For a long time now I have had a theory about Oisín and Tír na nÓg. I spent a recent weekend in Ballybunion at the opening of the Bachelor Festival and it was there that I found some concrete evidence to substantiate my proposition. Here's the way I see it.

Oisín and his father Fionn and a few more of the Fianna were one summer's evening indulging in one of their less-favourite pursuits, i.e., assisting in the saving of hay for one of the local farmers. The meadow in question would lie near the cross of Lisselton which is about halfway between Listowel and Ballybunion. Overhead there is a clear sky and a balmy breeze blows inland from nearby Atlantic seas. The time would be the latter end of June as they so quaintly put it in that part of the world. There is a blessed silence all over the meadow with every man committed to the task in hand.

Then suddenly out of the distance comes the thunder of hooves. The Fianna, no less fond of diversion than any other voluntary labourers, lean on their wooden rakes and pikes and wait for the horse and, hopefully, rider to come within their ken. They have not long to wait for in less time than it takes to say rum and blackcurrant they are confronted by the comeliest of maidens astride a snorting white charger.

No cap or cloak, as the song says, does this maiden wear but her long flowing tresses of burnished gold cover the sensitive areas of her beautifully shaped body. Sitting erect on her steed she surveys the menfolk all around and a doughty bunch they are, each man more robust and more handsome than the next. No interest does she evince as her blue eyes drift from face to face. Then her gaze alights on Oisín, poet, philosopher, charmer and athlete.

She surveys him for a long time before she gives him the come hither. He hesitates. Remember he is in the presence of his father and the like of Conan Maol.

"Come on," she says.

"Where?" asks Oisín.

"Tír na nÓg," says she.

"Go on, man," urge the Fianna in unison. No grudge do they bear him for such was the code of the Fianna. He hesitates no longer but throws his rake to one side and, with a mighty bound, lands himself behind her on the back of the magnificent white steed.

"Gup outa that," says she and the next thing you know they have disappeared altogether from view.

"Where did she say they were going?" old Fionn asks anxiously.

"Tír na nÓg," the others answered.

"It must be some land to the west of Ballybunion," the old chief surmises and without further ado he addresses himself to a swathe of hay.

The time went by and men and women went about their business. Then one day at that part of the Listowel-Ballybunion road known as Gortnaskeha the white horse reappeared bearing upon its back the handsome Oisín and the beautiful golden-haired woman. They came upon a number of men trying to move a large boulder from one side of the road to the other. All their efforts were in vain. They could not budge the boulder. Oisín leaned down from the horse and with his ludeen moved the great stone to one side but in so doing, poor chap, he fell forward on his face and eyes from his seat.

As he lay on the ground, exhausted and worn, the blonde spurred her horse and was never seen again in that part of the world although other blondes were to surface in Ballybunion with unfailing regularity year after year down to this very day and everyone of them as lovely as Niamh of the Golden Hair, which was the name of Oisín's partner.

Finding himself unable to rise he placed a hand on the shoulder of one of the Gortnaskeha men. "I've been in Tír na nÓg," he said.

"Tír na nÓg!" they exclaimed in wonder, for all had heard of it.

"Tír na nÓg my tail," said an old man with a dudeen in his mouth. "Ballybunion he's been to."

"But how did he age so much?" the others asked.

"Listen my friend," said the old man, "if you spent a weekend in Ballybunion with a blonde the like of what we saw on the white horse you'd have wrinkles too."

Which all goes to prove that a long weekend in Ballybunion can knock more out of a man than a score of years anywhere else.

A Typical Trip Down 42nd Street

In New York I walked down the 42nd Street stretch every other night on my way to the theatre where my play *Big Maggie* was showing. I could have taken a taxi but it was easier to walk and besides my wife, who was terrified of the place, wasn't with me so there was no need to look out for anybody but myself.

The secret of survival on 42nd Street at night is to keep your eyes wide open but to pretend that you're not in the least curious, that the area is familiar stamping ground. Don't look people between the eyes. Anything can happen. Walk on the edge of the pavement. Move briskly. Keep your hands out of your pockets and with luck no harm will befall you. Above all, don't spit. Nobody spits in New York. Anyway it's against the law.

One night while ambling innocently home from the theatre with an elderly relative we were accosted by a small, stout, black woman who eyed us speculatively for a split second before she spoke. She was a chunky sort of lady. In the rural Ireland of my boyhood she would probably have been termed a Dexter.

"You guys pussy-huntin'?" she asked.

"Naw," said my friend, "you got the wrong guys. We ain't huntin' for nothin'."

So saying he led the way into a topless bar where an anaemic if well-made young woman walked up and down a platform braless and with the skimpiest of panties. I wish I could say that she was dancing because that was what she was supposed to be doing. She did her slow-motion cavorting to loud music which came from a dark background where two men lounged against a dirty wall, bare, cracked and cobwebbed.

The girl reminded me of a caged animal. She advanced and retreated with glazed eyes, seeing nothing, saying nothing. The lady behind the counter was also topless and all but bottomless. The two beers ordered by my friend cost eight dollars.

"Let's get outa here," he said after one sip. "I seen enough." It transpired that he had spent forty-four years in New York and had always wanted to walk into a topless bar. What a time he chose and what a place!

Out on the strip young women pouted and older dames touted as did boys and young men. Debauchery was a way of life here. It was all strictly business, however. The streets reeked of prostitution but there was a basic innocence to much of it. The faces, most of them, were not far enough removed from childhood to be hardened properly. There was still something to salvage.

"Most of those dames do pretty well," my friend was saying. "They're dead beat at eighteen but they got the looks left and some have money so they con some guy and then live happy ever after which is maybe six or seven months or longer if they're lucky. Main thing is they get off the streets. The streets are for kids. They don't bruise so easily."

It was obvious that he took the whole business for granted. We crossed the street and walked down the other side. It was no different from the side we vacated except that it was a little darker and this is not so good. Sulky, hostile looks greeted us.

"I'll walk in front," my friend said, "you walk behind and don't worry. I gotta piece." This meant he had a gun. Maybe he had. Maybe he hadn't. The important thing was that he walked as though he had. He had spent the best part of his working life as a security man.

We reached the car park after what seemed an eternity. On our way to 44th Street we ran into what is probably New York's most recent and most unusual phenomenon. We stopped for a moment to watch a TV crew shooting some scenes at the base of George M. Cohan's monument but before we could take off again a black youth appeared from nowhere bearing a small window wiper and a squirter of water. His aim was to clean the car windscreen. Without as much as a by your leave he squirted the water and proceeded to wipe.

"Give the jerk a quarter," my friend said. This operation happens all the time in New York. More often than not the window is dirtier afterwards than it was before. Most people pay up on the grounds that it's better than being mugged and that at least the young window wipers are making an honest effort. Others adamantly refuse in spite of the fact that there's an outside chance of a broken windscreen. I've been in a car where the windscreens were wiped four times in the one night and all at the mangy cost of one dollar. It could only happen in New York.

Ham and Tomatoes

Whenever the security of the house where I was born was breached by unexpected visitors one of the family would be dispatched to a convenient grocery store for ham and tomatoes.

The rest of the ingredients would be in stock so to speak. The accepted practice of the period was to provide two slices of ham and one medium-sized tomato, halved, quartered or otherwise sliced, for each visitor.

Lettuce leaves and a few rings of raw onion were then added until one ran out of plate. This was looked upon as a substantial meal fit for clergy, Yanks or well-off relations. I don't know why the good folk of the period relied so heavily on ham and tomatoes. I daresay it was because ham was tenderer than any other form of cooked meat.

Also take into account the fact that it could be machine cut to suit any number of visitors. If there were too many the slices were naturally thinner although the remaining proportions, to wit, length and breadth, were mercifully the same and could be relied upon to mantle most of the plate provided there was no over-lapping and the other constituents were also of adequate dimensions.

The visitors would eat slowly taking only small mouthfuls but often there would be a rough and ready fellow who would let down the side by rolling a slice of ham over and over until he could fork it and transport it holus-bolus to the mouth. The second slice always met the same fate. He managed to give the impression that he had only been given two mouthfuls of ham. His ignorant actions cast a reflection on the household.

After the ham had been hastily masticated and consumed he would lick his chops like a mastiff and with a knife and fork upturned look around him eagerly for more.

Tomatoes, lettuce and onions failed to excite him. Indeed I saw a gentleman of this ilk having consumed his own portion of ham resort to the compulsory acquisition of another person's ham who in this case happened to be an elderly lady who had only proce-eded halfway through her first slice.

"Here," said he as he deftly removed the untouched slice with his fork, "I'll take this off your hands." Another favoured comment was, "You'll never eat all that; 'twill only sicken you."

Having devoured the slice of ham he cast about him seeking whatever slices he might devour.

On the credit side it could be said that he hastened the con-sumption of the comestibles so that the meal was finished quickly and the house left to its rightful occupants once more. Most visitors were possessed of a common trait and that was that while they might spend the greater part of the day embarrassing their hosts into providing a meal of sorts they immediately vamoosed as soon as the said meal was ingested.

There was a relation of ours, a withdrawn, unpretentious poor fellow, who would arrive in town unfailingly for the second day of Listowel Races. He would park his bicycle in our backyard, remove the clips from his trousers, comb his hair and politely refuse the offer of tea which had been made to him.

When the offer was repeated he might say, "All right so. I'll take a cup out of my hand."

This was to imply that he did not wish to inconvenience anybody, that he was utilising the minimum amount of ware, foregoing the use of a saucer and of a chair where he might, if he were less inconsiderate, roost for the day and be an encumbrance to everybody. The trouble with these models of self-effacement was that they looked upon the drinking of tea as a form of diversion rather than a means of sustenance.

·What a cup out of the hand meant in conventional terms was that the recipient recognised the need for some form of communication between himself and his relations but being retiring and bashful could do no more than "take tay" with them. The trouble was that he never knew when to take his leave and would often stand quietly for hours on end clutching his cup as though it were his only lifeline with the immediate world around him.

The most dangerous type of visitor is he who when invited to partake of a cup of tea announces firmly that he is only after "rising from the table". Very good if he presents himself with this fable at a time other than mealtime but if he arrives while a meal is in progress be certain that, given a second invitation, he will eat the unfortunate host out of house and home.

This has always been my experience with the man who has just risen from the table. To be fair to him, however, he has more or less laid his cards on the table which he now faces.

He does not say, "I could not look at a bite," as many others do who have completed a meal immediately prior to the invitation. He simply says, "I'm only just after rising from the table." Inherent, however, in this seemingly conclusive pronouncement is a warning for those who will heed it. The warning might well be worded like this, "I am truly after only rising from the table but this does not preclude me from sitting at another table if pressed to do so."

Watch out, therefore, for men who say they have just risen from the table for these are creatures of gluttonous and rapacious natures who cannot and will not make do with the produce of one table and who are forever on the lookout for invitations to partake of the produce of other tables.

Most sinister of all visitors and very often the most misleading is he who sits himself down and waits to be asked if he will partake of a cup of tea or a snack of some kind but who, when accepting the offer, does so conditionally.

"I will," he says, "if you are all having it." The implication here is that he does not consider himself a worthy enough guest to merit a meal or part of a meal on his own. He is simply suggesting that unless there is a meal in the offing as a matter of course that he will not accept it.

This is what he would like to imply but very often, alas, his message becomes garbled in transit and is quite often taken to mean this: "I will accept your kind offer to dine but only on condition that everybody else dines as well."

This display of magnanimity always endears him at once to those in attendance who are not regular members of the household. If his suggestion is enacted it is not those who provide the repast who are praised for their generosity and why should they be praised? Were it not for the conditional clause contained in the acceptance of the visitor there would have been nothing for anybody. Is it not logical, therefore, to give thanks to him rather than to the householders?

There are many houses where, because of abuses of the afore-mentioned nature, the householders are reluctant to be expansive when offering refreshment to visitors.

"Sure you won't have tea?" is a common safeguard employed by those who have been bitten too often in the past.

What this means is that the householder is more than willing to lay the table for tea even if the visitor has given the distinct impression that he is already overfed and in no need of tea.

It could also mean this: "You're far too high up in the world to consider seriously taking tea with the likes of us. Please don't embarrass us by accepting our humble fare."

Another suitable ploy is to stir up the fire until the flames induce the kettle to start singing. This should provoke the visitor into asking the following question: "I hope you're not boiling that kettle for me?"

Thus a tea-making situation is averted because he has implied that he does not wish the kettle to be boiled specially for him. He may, of course, if pressed, allow the kettle to be boiled for him but the tendency in this less hospitable day and age is not to provide tea unless it is specifically asked for.

There was a time in this much-abused land when there would be a mad rush to rinse out the teapot the moment a visitor was sighted on the roadway.

I hope our findings on this occasion will be of some assistance to those who have suffered more than their share from voracious visitors who depend largely on excursions to liberal households for their daily bread.

Great Dogs

My friend Davy Gunn, the bodhrawn-maker, once had a black dog who was one sixteenth part German shepherd, one sixteenth part greyhound, three sixteenths part beagle, three sixteenths part foxhound and the remaining sixteenths cocker spaniel.

In appearance, oddly enough, the Gunn dog bore no resemblance at all to the breeds in question. He was, instead, a dead ringer for a Labrador retriever. The dog's name was Esther which is a female name but because he was the only survivor of a large litter it was decided he should be called after his mother whose name happened to be Esther and who died in pupbirth.

According to Gunn, Esther was a remarkable dog. There was the time Gunn received a gift of puddings and porksteaks from a neighbour who had killed a pig. The first thing Gunn did upon receiving the puddings was to give the child who delivered them a half-crown.

The second thing he did was to put down the frying pan. He then selected a nicely turned, medium sized pudding and two juicy, mouth-watering strips of filleted pork. This was more than enough to satisfy the immediate needs of himself and his missus. Soon the heat made itself felt in the body of the pan and as it did the most appetising of smells and the most agreeable of sounds arose from the puddings and porksteaks. Gunn set the table after turning the pan's contents upside down so that both sides might benefit from the frying.

"The next thing that happened," we'll let Davy Gunn take over here, "was that Esther came into the kitchen and planked himself down in front of the range. Every time I tried to get near the pan he yowled and scowled and threatened to bite the hand off me. It wasn't like him at all. Normally he'd bite nothing, not even a fox or a rabbit he was that quiet. Finally I lay hoult of the coarse brush which happened to be standing outside the back door but all to no good for he refused to budge."

"I don't know in God's name what ails him," Davy Gunn's wife Maimie exclaimed.

"Wait a minute. Wait a minute," said Gunn. "What day have we?"

When no answer was forthcoming he went to the calendar and there his worst fears were confirmed.

"I declare to my goodness," said he, "if it isn't Friday."

In those days every Friday was a fast day and if a man broke the fast he'd have a mortal sin on top of his soul. The upshot of the ruction was that Gunn lured Esther away from the frying pan by the simple expedient of tossing a piece of unfried pudding out the front door. Esther was only canine, poor fellow, and could not resist the titbit.

"But I'll tell you one thing," said Gunn, "we did not touch the puddings and porksteak till after midnight that night when it was no sin to eat meat. I suppose you might say that the dog saved our souls."

"That reminds me," said a man from Gortnaminch who happened to be stationed nearby with a glass of lager in his hand. "'Tis a long time ago now since my father and myself and two other dogs went hunting one Sunday evening. We ruz three hares and killed one. We ruz a badger but he went to earth. What happened in the heel of the evening didn't the two dogs sit down and start to ullagone. They were like two ladies would be singing in an opera."

"Come on outa that, ye low hounds," my father shouted. Then the dogs stopped and we heard the Convent Bell from Listowel as clear as the wind in the heather.

"Them dogs is human," my father said.

"How come you make that out, Da?" I asked him.

"There's a men's mission closing tonight in Listowel," said he, "and if we start now we'll be there in time to renounce the devil."

"My great grandfather," said a Ballylongford man, "had a greyhound bitch one time and usen't she stand on her two front paws every time she heard the National Anthem."

"Go along, dang you," said Gunn, "there was no National Anthem in those days."

"What happened to Esther?" asked a young man from Ballybunion.

"Ah yes!" said Gunn sadly, "poor Esther! I had him with me driving in-calf heifers to Listowel cattle fair one morning when this Rolls Royce pulled up and a man with a grey head stuck his head out the window."

"Who owns the Labrador?" he asked in a grand accent.

"I'm the owner," said Gunn.

"Name your price," said the man with the grey head.

"He's not for sale," said Gunn.

"A hundred pounds," said the man with the grey head.

"That's different," said Gunn and he took the money.

"What about his papers?" the man with the grey head asked.

"Right here, my good man," said Gunn and he handed over a copy of ballad of Bould Thady Quille which happened to be in his breast pocket at the time.

"Wasn't that wrong?" said the man from Gortnaminch.

"Will you houl' until I finish," said Gunn. "I declare to God wasn't I going through the *News of the World* one Sunday evening when I came across this item on the back page. 'Irish dog wins first prize at Dangleton Dog Show' and there was Esther's photo and he smiling like he'd be after finding a parcel of chops. So you see," Gunn continued triumphantly, "if anyone was wronged it was me."

"Where is Dangleton?" the Gortnaminch man asked. Gunn laughed.

"A man who don't know where Dangleton is," said Gunn, "shouldn't be allowed to own a dog. 'Tis in the heart of England that's where it is and where else would it be I ask you except in that very spot?"

Gunn went on to tell us of how he missed Esther and how he regretted taking the hundred pounds from the man with the grey head even if it was an outrageous price.

"A man will never forget a good dog," said Davy Gunn. In the background someone with a Tarbert accent spoke a couplet from Kipling's 'The Power of the Dog':

Brothers and sisters I bid you beware
Of giving your heart to a dog to tear.

Several people in the bar told stories about their dogs, all beginning in the same way – "We had a dog once" – as they launched into improbable tales about these remarkable canines.

"They boast about dogs," said Gunn in an aside, "the way they boast about children."

When their tales were exhausted Davy Gunn took over again.

"I had a greyhound during the Economic War that polished off a calf a day," he said. "He grew to the the size of a wolfhound. In the end we could not keep him in meat and we gave him to a circus."

"What was the name of the circus?" the Gortnaminch man asked.

"I forget," Gunn replied wearily. "All I know is they painted this dog with black stripes and passed him off as a genuine tiger."

"I remember him," said the Gortnaminch man. "Had he a cut over his eye?"

"I don't know," said Gunn, "but if you don't stop asking questions you'll have a cut over your arse."

This chastened the Gortnaminch man and he asked no more questions. It transpired during the remainder of the discussions that several of those present had no dog. All had had dogs at one stage or another in their lives but for various reasons had given them up.

"A house without a dog," said Davy Gunn, "is like a hearth without a fire."

"Too true," said the Gortnaminch man as he made for the door, "and a house without a liar is like a hearse without a coffin."

Bicycles

Dan Paddy Andy O'Sullivan's famous dancehall at the cross of Renagown in the Stacks Mountains really flourished right through the fifties when young bucks driving motor cars arrived on the scene for the first time to initiate its decline. The conveyances were generally Baby Fords or Ford Prefects. Sometimes there would be a fourteen point nine pick-up but whatever make they were they were harbingers of doom for the old ways in the Stacks.

One night Dan Paddy Andy came on the stage between dances and made one of his famous announcements. Cars had been arriving to the hall in increasing numbers. Their drivers rarely came to dance. They came to make pick-ups.

"In this hall," said Dan, "if a man wants to make out a woman he better have a stink of petrol off him."

The bicycle, so long the mistress of the rural road, was to be consigned to a secondary role. No more would young country lads bar their girls home from dances nor would the night wind sing in their ears as they rode free-wheel downdale.

Dan Paddy Andy was right. A smell of petrol was what the young women wanted. The twirl of car keys in the hand of a townie meant so much more than the bicycle clips which are now no more than museum pieces. In the end the bicycle became an anachronism as far as going to dancehalls was concerned.

It was, for generations, an object of reverence and often the sole topic of discussion among young people. Then came the dynamo lamp and the three speed gear and it became the most prized possession of every country household.

Its maintenance was a priority. There was no finer diversion than the tuning up of a bike of a winter's night. It wasn't just diversion for the self-taught mechanic. It provided entertainment for the whole household. There they would sit, in a circle around the hearth, their faces turned outward to witness the oiling and polishing of the upturned machine.

One of the younger members of the family might be permitted to spin the pedals so that the wheels hummed, pinged and chimed, whirred and whistled and whined until the maximum number of revolutions had been reached. Then there was only one sustained, near-to-silent supersound as the wheels spun in a blinding silver dazzle. No one would dare speak while the bike held forth and its proprietor stood proudly to one side so that the world might share the wonder that was his bicycle.

In those days it was all right for a man to ride a women's bicycle but for a woman to mount a man's bicycle was regarded as highly unladylike. All right for young girls maybe in their early teens but for older girls or especially women it was not the done thing.

In my humble estimation there was nothing in the world as beautiful as a well turned-out bicycle especially on a summer's day when cooling breezes fanned the cyclist and the seashore beckoned. When Dan Paddy Andy announced that a smell of petrol was necessary for the attracting of bright young things in the Renagown dancehall he was mourning the passing of a way of life.

While the motor car was good to Dan the bicycle had been better. Dan availed of the passing motor to travel to places like

Castleisland, Tralee and Listowel when horse and cattle fairs were being held in those towns. Perversely, however, the motor car took away his most prized patrons to the same towns to all-night dances and other diversions which had been outside the range of the cyclist.

It could, therefore, be said that the motor car closed the Renagown dancehall as it did most other small country halls and places such as platforms and crossroads where traditionally dancing was held.

Another favourite pastime in the Stacks in those distant days was the pelting of passing cyclists at night with clods and cadhrawns, i.e., small sods of turf. Townies were always regarded as fair game, especially if they were chaps who incurred local wrath by monopolising the best-looking girls at the local dancehall.

Sometimes from the cover of a hedge there would be a shower of clods and cadhrawns on the heads and shoulders of a squad of home-going townies. There was little outcry since townies always wore caps and coats and it was also generally conceded that they had exceedingly hard heads.

Human Hibernation

It is a source of constant amazement to me in a world filled with massage parlours, saunas, keep fit studios and weight-reducing classes that there is not, to my knowledge, a single hibernation unit.

It is left to the noble bear to represent the upright creatures of the earth in the process known as hibernation. The bear, who is less intelligent than man, according to man, is capable of shedding half of his body fat by the simple expedient of retiring to a cave and sleeping it off. The only thing man sleeps of is an overdose of booze.

During the most recent cold spell, however, I had my first experience of human hibernation. I found myself waking up later in the day than ever before and while this extended sojourn in the land of Nod might be in some small way due to the arrival of middle age I feel, nevertheless, that the frosty weather out of doors must shoulder most of the blame.

As the cold spell wore on I slept longer and longer until, eventually, I spent a whole day in bed snoozing, snoring, snorting and relaxing. I declined all offers of food from a concerned spouse and spurned offers of daily newspapers from equally concerned offspring. I arose from my couch late that night, swallowed two pints of beer and ate a quarter pound of Cheddar cheese together with five crackers before retiring again.

I followed the same procedure the next day but that night I remained on in bed and neither ate nor drank. The following morning when I weighed myself I discovered to my delight that I had lost seven pounds. My paunch which had tended to protrude of late had almost completely disappeared whilst the blackening ravines beneath my optics had vanished without trace. I decided to spend another whole day and night in bed without eating or drinking.

I concentrated on sleep and while it was fitful enough to begin with I nodded off after a while and remained suspended in a somnolent state for several hours. I had earlier warned my family that nothing was amiss, that I was simply sleeping off my excess fat. Towards evening I arose and weighed myself to discover that I was eleven pounds lighter and feeling none the worse after my sleeping session. The pounds had gone and I had not been obliged to confine myself to fat-destroying pills or to a particular diet or to physical exercise. All I did was copy the bear and indulge in a spot of hibernation. My paunch had completely disappeared and my complexion, ever indebted for its ruddiness to a plentiful intake of beer and an abiding love of the outdoors, had improved enormously.

The question arose in my mind as to why mankind is not given to hibernating as a means of losing weight. The bear does it with no ill-effects, often in a damp cave with nothing to cover him but leaves. Man has central heating, warm beds, electric blankets and hot water bottles and yet he refuses to hibernate for more than a half day at a time.

The following week the cold came again and I decided to spend a few more days in bed having first seen to my numerous obligations. Again I slept fairly soundly, never waking before one o'clock until late in the third day of hibernation I was visited by a delegation which consisted of most of my family.

118

I recalled that the last time such a delegation had visited me I had gone off the booze for a few weeks. They had maintained then that I should return to my old drinking habits straight away. When I declined they were quick to point out that as bad as I was making things for myself I was making them even worse for them.

"On the drink," they said, "we can just about tolerate you. Off the drink you are teetotally unbearable."

During the latest representation they pointed out that I should abandon my so-called hibernation on the grounds that it was upsetting the whole household.

I yielded. But if there is anybody reading this who suffers from obesity let me recommend the hibernation gambit as a safe and painless method of losing weight. It is a shame that there are no hibernation parlours where the overweight might submit themselves to uninterrupted dozing and slumber for a prolonged period. To me it seems a perfectly natural thing to do and with his superior intelligence man should surely be able to hibernate better than the bear. In one's own home it costs nothing and think of all those disappearing pounds without resort to tasteless diets and exhausting exercises.

Extraordinary Language

Ordinary language is something I can do without. By this I mean nattering and muttering and the likes. Blunt responses, bleak descriptions and blank statements all depress me if they are not frequently enlightened by bright interjections. It all adds up to the fact that thousands and thousands of unemployed words and even greater numbers of aborted sentences which might have cheered the world will never be called into service. This is why I always seek the company of men and women who are never satisfied to express themselves in an ordinary, run-of-the-mill manner.

I accept, of course, that nobody must be denied the right to express themselves in ordinary language but how infinitely more colourful our lives might be made by eccentric, unconventional or even freakish language. I would outlaw foul language although I can understand the need for it when frustration is so demoralising that all other language seems inadequate.

In my time it has been my good fortune to have met up with men and women to whom everyday language is anathematical. Their philosophy would seem to be that if it cannot be said in an unusual or at least a different way then it should not be said at all. They deserve great credit for this. There is no material reward and there is often the danger of abusive language in return. Not so very long ago a great word artist passed on but so modest was he that were I to publicly credit him with the least of his observations he would probably rise from the dead or, at the very least, turn over in his grave.

I remember once he told me that he happened to be working in a farmer's house when, for his midday meal, he was presented with a plate of bacon and cabbage. The bacon, alas, was fat and if there was one nutrient to which our friend's digestive tract was allergic it was fat bacon. There are others who are partial to fat bacon but they are few in number. Lean bacon is loved by many but mixed or streaky bacon is loved by all. However, let us press on!

"Was it all fat?" I asked knowing that he would embroider his reply with some uncommon verbiage.

"There was not as much lean in it as you'd draw with a stroke of a red biro."

Another time he was endeavouring to correct a faulty chimney in an ancient cottage in the heart of the countryside. When he arrived at the pub that evening he was covered with grime.

"The white is gone from you altogether," said a wag who happened to be in attendance.

"Ah," said our friend, "you should see the woman of the house where I was working. She never stirred outside the door all day and in the heel of the evening she was looking like she'd be after a month in Morocco."

"What about the children?" asked the wag. "Were they brown too?".

"Brown!" echoed the tradesman. "I only saw one child there and he was the nearest thing you ever saw to a kipper."

Once he was in court as a witness and decided that it might not be amiss if he were to tank up with a mixture of stout and whiskey to make the proceedings more bearable. This is common practice in most court districts in Ireland and often one is assailed by the odour of whiskey and stout in the body of the court. The court in question was of the circuit variety and the judge wore a wig. When our friend was in the box giving evidence the solicitor who happened to be cross-questioning him announced that he could only barely hear him.

"Speak up," said the judge.

"All right missus," our friend replied.

"Address the court properly or I'll have you in contempt," said the judge.

"I will. I will," said our friend, "but is it miss or missus I'll call you?"

I could go on but I think I have made the point and that is that the world is a richer place because of those who eschew the mediocre in matters vocal and who seek new designs and patterns for their various locutions.

The Irish Political Scene

It might be more appropriate to label this treatise "Of Cats and Dogs" and I'll tell you why. Some time ago in Dáil Éireann as Mr. Dukes, the Finance Minister, was announcing the unprecedented increase in the price of dog licenses, a Fianna Fail deputy asked, "What about cats?"

I don't know who the deputy was. The papers didn't say. He spoke in jest but his timely interjection should not be allowed to die without comment. At the time of writing we Irish are not obliged to license our cats and I am mystified that no government has made cat licensing obligatory over the years.

Could it be that because cats have nine lives their owners

would be expected to pay nine times the amount paid for dogs? Could it be that cats would be difficult to identify, especially at night when all cats are said to be grey? Could it be that a government might fear the backlash of ridicule after proposing the licensing of cats or is it simply that politicians are fonder of cats than they are of dogs? Could it be that politicians are afraid of cats? A black cat brings luck but heaven alone knows what calamitous misfortune a licensed cat might bring. Could it be that politicians love cats?

The answer to all these questions is no. The truth is that governments are death down on farmers and dogs. These preposterous obsessions are inexplicable but true. They should be ashamed of themselves for without the farmer we would starve and is not the dog man's best friend?

Why then have we the disgraceful spectacle of a countryside filled with cowering dogs and fearful farmers whilst the cat may roam free and accountable to no master? The cat would seem to be the tax evader of the animal world. It is no longer good enough to say, "More power to him," or to his human counterpart.

Remember that a cat has no loyalty, not even to other cats. A dog on the other hand will very often lay down his life for his master and although we kick our dogs and scold our dogs their loyalty is always guaranteed.

In many ways the situation regarding cats and dogs reminds me of the political scene that obtains in Ireland. Why is the farmer who feeds us unfailingly forever on the defensive and why does the noble dog continually hang his faithful head? Loyalty is taxed while the perfidious and disobedient may howl, growl and snarl at will. They snap at the heels of their masters while those who blindly lick the feet of those self-same masters are thrown by the wayside.

Is this proper recompense for a lifetime of tail-wagging and fawning? Is this the reward for running after and recovering a thousand sticks? Is this to be the thanks for retrieving the carelessly cast stones of their overlords? What is the penalty for unwittingly returning with the wrong stick or the wrong stone? The answer is banishment forever. There are many TD's who will bear me out.

And what of the farmer? Has he yet starved or deprived us? No indeed. Always he has kept the wolf from our door and yet whenever his name is mentioned the saliva runs down the jowls of the aforementioned wolf at the prospect of a kill. I have never seen anybody so agitated as a trade unionist at the mention of farmers' tax. I have seen these very same trade unionists time after time on television close their eyes as other game passes safely by but the minute the unfortunate farmer hoves into view the demented yelping begins and the pack takes off. Talk about biting the hand that feeds them!

For cats roam free, aided and abetted by the laws of the land. Tomcats and pussycats tread the primrose paths of dalliance, unrebuked and unchastened, puling and ullagoning at all hours while the faithful hound maintains his thankless vigil at the door of his master. While cats rove sex-crazed under changing moons, the hound stands firm and faithful.

Is loyalty no longer a virtue? Alas it would seem not and it would seem that the chief of modern virtues is not being found out. If all that has been politically concealed in recent times is ever revealed there will be hell to pay but there is as much hope of this happening as there is of a tax on cats. Politically speaking, of course, cats aren't the only ones with nine lives.

Going, Going, Gone

Thursday morning, time eleven forty-five. Back along the street which leads to Ballybunion I have an unrestricted view. I have been here for more than an hour sitting by the window vainly seeking inspiration. This has happened a hundred times before. Often I was on the verge of despair and would be about to pack up my traps when God would reveal Himself in the most unexpected way.

All morning I have been exploring new avenues without success. Upon beholding rain clouds forming to the west I was reminded of Housman's immortal lines, at least I think it was Housman. I had intended to go for a long walk this afternoon but it looks as if I will have to change my plans. How's that Housman puts it?

Loud quack the ducks, the peacocks cry,
The distant hills are looking nigh.
The walls are damp, the ditches smell,
Closed is the pink-eyed pimpernel.
'Twill surely rain I see with sorrow,
Our jaunt must be put off till tomorrow.

Those few couplets are but random extracts. I cannot recall the entire poem and indeed if I could I dare not include it since my brief is to entertain as best I can with witty and original material.

But wait, what figure from a distant shop emerges? I know him well, a fellow of infinite laziness, a handyman of sorts. You might say that he is a client of this institution, not a regular one mark you but one given to the occasional extended visit. He bears in his extended hands several rolls of wallpaper and yet manages to consult his watch. He pauses and looks from his battered car to these premises. He is struggling with himself it is plain to be seen. He looks upwards and notes the darkened heavens. He goes to his car, opens it, deposits the wallpaper and once more consults his watch. He closes the door of the car and stands in the centre of the street with folded arms. I know what's the matter. He is on the verge of making a decision but needs guidance. Like myself he trusts in God and knows that God's will is sure to manifest itself in God's good time.

No sign, however, is forthcoming. He stands there and looks to left and right as if in these areas he might find the revelation he requires. He looks before him and he looks behind him still unable to resolve his problem. He looks upwards again and shakes his head, an intimation this that he is no lover of rain and yet it is plain to be seen that he is prepared to let it rain.

Once more towards these premises he directs his eyes and casts a longing, lingering look thereon. He has almost reached a decision. He inserts his right hand into his trousers pocket and locates his keys. He extracts them and looks towards his car. He twirls the keys expertly on his forefinger and looks here, there and everywhere.

"Going!" his every gesture says.

He twirls the keys secondly and looks at my pub once more.

"Going!" his gestures repeat the word. He allows a decent interval to pass before bringing down the hammer. Again he looks here, there and everywhere only this time he does so with absolute thoroughness. He clutches the keys in the palm of his hand and moves towards his car.

"Gone!" his every gesture says. It is a small thing that would have turned him. Although my premises is the loser, I am glad that wallpapering has won the day. There is no day like a wet day for wallpapering. This then is how another contribution comes to be written. By simple but dedicated observation and by faith and the goodness of God we have achieved our aim.

The rain has begun to fall and I recall that last evening's sunset was pale pink rather than red. This is always a sure indication of rain. As I recall, however, the poet put it somewhat better than your humble servant when he recalled how

Last night the sun went pale to bed
The moon in halo hid her head.

ALSO PUBLISHED BY BRANDON

MAN OF THE TRIPLE NAME
by John B. Keane

"This lyrical, most human and highly humorous book." – Benedict Kiely, *The Irish Times*.
"Anybody who enjoys old-style storytelling at its best should reach for *Man of the Triple Name*." – *Irish Post*.
"Highly enjoyable." – *In Dublin*.
"Fascinating." – *Limerick Leader*.
"Hilarious social history." – *Boston Irish News*.

Hardback ISBN 0 86322 046 0   Paperback ISBN 0 86322 061 4

GREEN AND GOLD
The Wrenboys of Dingle
by Steve MacDonogh

"A heartening and very readable account . . . and a valuable historical document . . . liberally sprinkled with excellent photographs." – "Folkland," *RTE Radio 1*.
"Amusing, informative and full of local flavour." – *Ireland's Own*.
"Quite an accomplishment . . . Brandon have paid a handsome homage to their place of location." – *Drogheda Independent*.

Hardback ISBN 0 86322 040 1   Paperback ISBN 0 86322 041 X

Published by Brandon Book Publishers Ltd., Cooleen, Dingle, Co. Kerry.